EDDIE KANTAR TEACHES
Topics in Declarer Play at Bridge

MASTER POINT PRESS • TORONTO

EDDIE KANTAR TEACHES
Topics in Declarer Play at Bridge

EDDIE KANTAR

Master Point Press
331 Douglas Ave
Toronto, Ontario Canada
M5M 1H2
(416) 781 0351
www.masterpointpress.com

Canadian Cataloguing in Publication Data
Kantar, Edwin B., 1932-
Eddie Kantar teaches topics in declarer play at bridge

Includes index
ISBN 1-894154-53-3

1. Contract bridge. I. Title.

GV1282.435.K35 2002   795.41'53   C2002-901836-6

Editor   Ray Lee
Cover   Olena Sullivan
Author photograph   Shireen Mohandes

Printed and bound in Canada by Webcom Ltd.

Introduction

It's always been my dream to write a book on the play of the hand. After all, I have made enough mistakes in the play over the years to cover two books!

Now my goal is to help you avoid some of these errors. After all, you want to instill enough trust in your partner so that he or she will let you play a hand once in a while! The problem is that each topic is so vast, that I can't imagine any writer doing justice to the major elements of the play of the hand in one volume that could be lifted by the average person.

The idea here is to try to teach you how to think and what to think about. Unless you have a clear-cut vision of how to organize the play you will inevitably find yourself in the wrong hand, lacking an entry to this or that hand, finding the dangerous opponent on lead at embarassing moments, or seeing winners disappear because of a blocked suit that wasn't unblocked in time! Accordingly I have decided to divide up the important topics into more than one book and go into each topic thoroughly so as not to short change the reader.

This is my opening bid, so to speak. I hope you like it.

Eddie Kantar

Contents

A Transport of Delight

"Oh, how I long to travel back."

HENRY VAUGHAN

An entry, an entry, my kingdom for an entry! How many times have you wished for just one more entry either to your hand or to dummy? Maybe that wish will be answered after reading this chapter. There are many, many techniques for preserving, creating, or forging entries to one hand or the other. Let's start with one of the most fertile areas for entry conservation and entry creation — your trump suit.

Drawing trumps — back and forth mobility

When you can draw trumps and still have at least one trump left both in your hand and in dummy, try to use those trumps to move back and forth — i.e. strive for 'entry flexibility'.

Translation: *being able to enter either hand with a trump whenever possible. Look at this typical situation:*

North
◊ Q 4 3

West
◊ 9 2

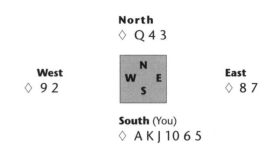

East
◊ 8 7

South (You)
◊ A K J 10 6 5

Diamonds are trumps and you plan to draw two rounds ending in your hand. If you start with the ace and king, you leave the blank ◊Q in dummy. Yes, you will then be able to cross to dummy with a diamond, but if you are in dummy with another suit, you can't enter your hand with a diamond; the suit is blocked. However, if you start with the ace and jack, again leaving the blank ◊Q in dummy, you have entry flexibility; you can zip over to dummy with a diamond, and if you are in dummy with another suit, you can overtake the queen with your king to get to your hand.

The beauty (and horror) of a powerful trump suit

The stronger your trump suit, the harder it may be to enter dummy with a trump; too many riches. One way to overcome this glut is to trump high, not low, when forced to ruff. Deuces and treys can be the most precious cards in your hand — cherish them; save them!

NORTH-SOUTH VUL. DEALER SOUTH

West	North	East	South
			2♣
pass	2◊	pass	2♠
pass	3♠	pass	4♣
pass	4♠	all pass	

North
♠ 6 5 4 3
♡ 8 6 4
◊ K Q J
♣ 8 6 5

South (You)
♠ A K Q J 10 2
♡ 10 7
◊ A
♣ A J 4 3

You do well to stop at 4♠ and the opponents start with three rounds of hearts. If you ruff with the deuce (a truly ugly play), you will have squandered the most precious card in your hand. That ♠2 is your entrée to dummy. If you ruff the third heart high, you can draw trumps, cash the ◇A, enter dummy with a trump, and discard two clubs on the diamonds. Ten tricks. If you ruff low at Trick 3, you could wind up losing two clubs along with the two hearts you have already lost.

Creating an extra dummy entry with your heart in your mouth

In the previous example, you had to ruff high in order to be able to enter dummy with a trump. Sometimes you have to get to dummy twice in the trump department when there only appears to be one trump entry to dummy. Appearances can be deceiving.

North
♠ 5 4 3
♡ J 9
◇ J 10 5
♣ Q 8 5 4 2

South (You)
♠ A Q J
♡ A K Q 4 3 2
◇ A K Q
♣ 7

This time your enthusiasm knows no bounds (bidding deleted so that you will continue reading this book) and you arrive at a contract of 6♡. West leads a diamond which you cleverly win in your hand. You have a certain club loser and you must find the ♠K with East to have any chance, so assume it is there. However, even if East has the ♠K, you probably will need two dummy entries to take two spade finesses. Do you see two dummy entries?

Your best chance to create a second dummy entry lies in the trump suit. At Trick 2, lead a low heart and stick in the nine! If it wins, you have two dummy entries to take two spade finesses. If the finesse loses, cheer up; if you normally pick up this kind of hand, going down is only a temporary setback. Besides, you took the right line of play. And if the ♡9 wins, but the spade finesse loses — isn't bridge a wonderful game?

More desperation plays

On the topic of 'desperation' finesses, let's not overlook a few others.

If you absolutely have to get to dummy twice in clubs, lead low to the jack, hoping West has the queen and doesn't play it. If West plays the queen, you can only get to dummy once. Don't worry, West isn't going to play the queen unless it drops out of his hand by mistake — or you are sitting too close to the table.

Another character-building finesse

Here's another scary situation. If you have to get to dummy twice in clubs, lead low to the ten, playing West for the jack. Just do it!

Now that bravery has set in, perhaps you are ready to deal with another 'entryless' dummy.

North
♠ 8 7 6 5
♡ 10 4
♢ 9 7 6 5
♣ A K Q

South (You)
♠ A 9 2
♡ A K Q 6 3 2
♢ A 8 4 2
♣ —

	NEITHER VUL.		DEALER SOUTH
West	**North**	**East**	**South**
			1♡
pass	1NT	pass	3♢
pass	3♡	pass	3♠
pass	4♣	pass	4♡
all pass			

This time you are in 4♡ and the opening lead is the ♠Q (couldn't they have led a club?). There you are, staring at the ♣AKQ with no way to get there. Not so fast. See that ♡10? If West has the ♡J and you lead a low heart from your hand, West cannot prevent you from getting to dummy with the ♡10 to discard three losing diamonds on those three lovely clubs. It's not a bad tradeoff: one heart for them, three clubs for you. And what if East has the ♡J? You're not supposed to ask questions like that.

Forcing a dummy entry

Here's another strange looking play that allows you to exchange a non-existent loser and get back two or more winners in return.

North
♠ 9 8 3
♡ A K Q 6
♢ 7 4 2
♣ 8 6 5

South
♠ A K Q J 6 4
♡ —
♢ K 9 6
♣ A Q 7 2

	NEITHER VUL.		DEALER SOUTH
West	**North**	**East**	**South**
			2♣
pass	2♡	pass	2♠
pass	3♠	pass	4♣
pass	4♡	pass	4♠
all pass			

You stop at 4♠ and West leads the ◊Q to East's ace. East returns a diamond to your king. On a good day, you might take the rest of the tricks. Say you bang down the ace and king of spades and the ♠10 drops, allowing you to enter dummy with the ♠9. Perfect. You can discard a diamond and two clubs on the hearts, take a winning club finesse, and blame partner for not bidding a cold slam.

Not so fast! What if the ♠10 doesn't drop? What if one defender started with ♠10xx? Now even a crowbar won't get you to dummy's hearts and you could actually go down on this hand! You could lose two diamonds and possibly two clubs, and then you would, of course, blame partner for bidding too much.

The answer is to make sure you get to dummy to use those beautiful hearts. Play the ♠A at Trick 3. If the ♠10 doesn't appear, lead a *low* spade to the eight, conceding an unnecessary trump loser, but forcing a dummy entry with the ♠9. Once you have a trump entry, you can use it to get rid of three of your minor suit losers on the hearts.

The First Trick

If all the contracts that were lost by overlooking entry problems (frequently at Trick 1) were laid end to end, there would be no end.

A recurring problem is where to win a trick when it can be taken in either hand. The idea is to 'advance the play' — play through your intended line in your head, asking yourself in which hand a later entry will be most needed. Once you do that, the proper play will flow from your fingers.

Advancing the play

North
♠ A Q 10 3 2
♡ A 3 2
◊ A 2
♣ 10 3 2

```
    N
  W   E
    S
```

South (You)
♠ 5
♡ K 7 4
◊ K J 10 4 3
♣ 9 7 6 4

NORTH-SOUTH VUL. DEALER SOUTH

West	North	East	South
			pass
pass	1♠	pass	1NT
all pass			

You deal and pass, partner opens 1♠ and your 1NT response ends the auction. The opening lead is the ♡J.

Before rushing to judgement, look at the entire hand. Count your sure tricks outside of your best suit, diamonds, to determine how many diamond tricks you need. You have three sure tricks outside of diamonds, the ♠A and the ♡AK, so you need to play diamonds for four tricks.

It is vital to preserve *later* entries to the hand that you are establishing. After all, you might just want to get back to that hand to cash the tricks you have set up. With that thought in mind, win the ♡A and play the ace and a diamond to the jack. Even if this loses, you have the ♡K as a re-entry to your established diamonds. If you win the ♡K at Trick 1 (gruesome), and then take a diamond finesse which loses (just desserts), you will be unable to get back to your hand to score your three established diamonds. Pity.

Ruffing Losers in the Dummy

If your plan is to ruff losers in the dummy, it's not a bad idea to have as many convenient hand entries as possible so you can return to your hand to ruff your losers before the opponents wise up and lead a trump.

EAST-WEST VUL.		DEALER SOUTH	
West	**North**	**East**	**South**
			1♡
pass	2♡	pass	4♡
all pass			

North
♠ K 6 4 3
♡ Q 7 5
◇ 6
♣ J 7 6 4 2

South
♠ A 9 5
♡ A J 8 6 3 2
◇ A J 9
♣ 8

Against silent opposition you wind up in 4♡. The opening lead is the ♠Q.

You would like to ruff two diamonds in dummy before drawing trumps. Let's advance the play. Say you win the ♠A, play the ◇A and ruff a diamond. How are you going to get back to your hand to ruff your last diamond? If you lead a club and East wins and plays a trump, you are in trouble. If you win the ♡A and ruff a diamond with the ♡Q, you could lose two trump tricks. If you duck East's heart play and West wins and returns a heart, you can no longer ruff your last diamond in dummy. You stand to lose a trick in each suit.

The answer is not to let them in to lead a heart. Win the opening lead in dummy (key play), play the ace and ruff a diamond, return to your hand with the ♠A (a beloved 'return entry'), ruff your last diamond, and play, the ♡Q, running it if it is not covered. With normal breaks you stand to lose a club, a spade, and probably a heart.

Don't be greedy

Another Trick 1 problem involving entries is resisting temptation, otherwise known as 'greed'. Greed can keep one from seeing the forest for the trees. The best way to defeat these two lurking devils is to *look at the entire hand and advance the play before playing to Trick 1.*

North
♠ Q
♡ A 10 8 6 2
◇ A K Q J 2
♣ K J

South (You)
♠ K 10 6 4
♡ 3
◇ 7 6 5
♣ A 5 4 3 2

| NEITHER VUL. | | DEALER NORTH | |
West	**North**	**East**	**South**
	1♡	pass	1♠
pass	3◇	pass	3NT
all pass			

After partner opens 1♡, you try 1♠, partner leaps to 3◇, and your 3NT rebid ends the auction. West leads the ♣6. What is your plan?

It helps to count sure tricks before playing to the first trick. If you don't, all the bridge books in the world, including this one, won't save you. You have five diamonds, two clubs, and one heart for eight tricks. It should be easy enough to establish a ninth trick in spades... providing you have a way to get to your hand to use it.

In other words, win the ♣K in dummy, and lead the ♠Q, driving out the ♠A. Your ♠K is your ninth trick and your ♣A is the entry to use it. If you play the ♣J at Trick 1 and East produces the ♣Q, call 911 because you're in big trouble.

Winning a trick with a higher card than necessary is yet another way to foil greed, particularly when it deals with getting to a long suit in dummy. On the following hand a non-greedy play saves you four tricks!

BOTH VUL.		DEALER NORTH	
West	**North**	**East**	**South**
	2◊	pass	2NT
pass	3♡[1]	pass	3NT
all pass			

1. Heart stopper and a maximum.

North
♠ 7 6 2
♡ Q 10 8
◊ K Q J 10 9 2
♣ 2

West
♠ K 10 4
♡ K J 7 6 2
◊ 3
♣ K 9 8 4

East
♠ Q 5 3
♡ 4 3
◊ A 8 7 6 4
♣ J 10 5

South (You)
♠ A J 9 8
♡ A 9 5
◊ 5
♣ A Q 7 6 3

The Rule of Eleven:

Subtract the card led from 11. This tells you the number of higher cards outstanding not in the opening leader's hand. In this deal where a six is led, and you can see five higher cards between your hand and dummy's, it is clear that East has no heart higher than the six.

This rule only works if the lead is fourth best.

After partner opens a vulnerable weak 2◊, you arrive at 3NT. The opening lead is a stubborn ♡6. The Rule of Eleven tells you that East has no card in hearts higher than the six. It looks as if you can take the trick cheaply with dummy's eight or your nine if you wish. Sure enough, when you play the ♡8 from dummy, East plays the ♡2. Steady. If you win this trick with a low card, how do you plan to get to dummy's diamonds after you knock out the diamond ace?

The idea is to use those diamonds, not be left staring at them longingly. Your only prayer of an entry is the ♡Q, but in order for the ♡Q to be an entry, you have to win the opening lead with the ♡A. Now you can drive out the ◊A and later lead a heart to the queen. Try making this hand if you win the first trick with any card other than the ace. Try going down three!

Ducking to preserve a hand entry

If the opening lead is about to knock out a valuable hand or dummy entry, there is no rule that says you have to take the trick; ducking the trick may preserve the entry for later.

North
♠ A K 6 5 4
♡ Q 6
♢ Q J 3
♣ A K 8

West
♠ Q 9
♡ A 9 2
♢ 10 9 8 6
♣ J 9 7 2

East
♠ J 10 8 7
♡ 8 7 5 3
♢ K 7 2
♣ Q 10

South (You)
♠ 3 2
♡ K J 10 2
♢ A 5 4
♣ 6 5 4 3

EAST-WEST VUL.		DEALER WEST	
West	**North**	**East**	**South**
pass	1♠	pass	1NT
pass	3NT	all pass	

You arrive at the best contract of 3NT and West leads the ◊10. You cover with the jack and East produces the king. Should you take the trick? Only if you want to go down in an ice-cold contract.

Look at the whole hand and form a plan. (Even a miserable plan is better than no plan.) Your security blanket starts by counting sure tricks outside of your best suit, hearts. You have two spades, two clubs and two diamonds. Hearts can easily be established for three tricks, by leading the queen, driving out the ace, and then taking the K-J-10. Of course, if they take the queen you have no problem. But what if they duck the queen and win the second heart lead instead? Will you be able to get to your hand for those two established hearts? You will if you duck the opening lead and win the likely diamond continuation in dummy. Now start hearts while you still have the ◊A tucked away safely in your hand; nothing can stop you.

Repeatable finesses

A **repeatable finesse** is another way of saying you may have to take two or three finesses in the same suit. This may, in turn, mean getting back to one hand two or even three times to take those finesses. 'Getting back' means entries, and entries mean planning.

North
♣ A Q J 10

West
♣ K 9 7 6

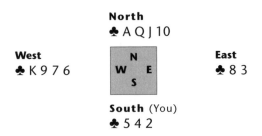

East
♣ 8 3

South (You)
♣ 5 4 2

Say the lead is in your hand and your goal is to take four club tricks. Given the diagram position, you will have to lead clubs three times from your hand. This means two additional hand entries. If the lead is in dummy, you need three hand entries to pick up the suit. Do not squander entries when you are staring down the barrel of a repeatable finesse.

EAST-WEST VUL.		DEALER NORTH	
West	**North**	**East**	**South**
	pass	pass	1♠
pass	1NT	pass	3♠
pass	4♠	all pass	

North
♠ 5 3
♡ A Q J 5
◇ 7 5 3 2
♣ 9 5 2

South (You)
♠ A K Q J 10 6
♡ 7 3
◇ Q 8 6
♣ A J

Here you open 1♠ (you get beautiful suits in this chapter) and partner bids 1NT. You toy with raising to 3NT, but you've seen this partner play before, so you settle for the cowardly rebid of 3♠; partner ups the ante to 4♠, West leads the ♣K and there you are.

Clearly you need to find West with the ♡K, but even so, you need to repeat the finesse to secure three tricks from the suit — what you need to make the contract. Repeating the heart finesse means returning to your hand *without letting the opponents in.*

See the trap? If you draw trumps and take a winning heart finesse, you can't get off dummy to repeat the finesse. You will be forced to come off dummy with a club (or a diamond). Now you are at grave risk of losing three diamonds and a club. The answer is **not** to draw trumps. Use your trump suit as your segue to your hand. Win the ♣A, take the heart finesse, return to your hand, drawing all of the outstanding trumps, and repeat the heart finesse. You will discard a minor suit loser on the ♡A, your tenth trick.

Timeout
Because entries are so critical when repeatable finesses are on the horizon, you have to know how to milk certain suits for the maximum number of entries.

Using entries to the weak hand intelligently

Ideally, the strength between your hand and dummy will be rather equally divided. If it is, it is easier to travel merrily back and forth from one hand to the other. However, if one hand has most of the strength, you had better do something worthwhile when the lead is in the weaker hand, because you may not get back there again until the next hand.

North
♠ 8 6 4
♡ 10 2
◇ A K Q J 9 8
♣ A J

South (You)
♠ A 7 3
♡ Q J 8
◇ 4 3 2
♣ Q 9 8 3

NEITHER VUL.		DEALER NORTH	
West	**North**	**East**	**South**
	1◇	1♠	1NT
pass	3NT	all pass	

With neither side vulnerable, partner opens 1◇, East throws in a 1♠ overcall, you try 1NT, and partner raises to 3NT. West leads the ♠10, East overtakes with the ♠J, and you win the spade continuation with the ace, West following. Now what?

Count tricks. You have eight sure tricks: six diamonds, one spade, and one club. You can settle for down one by running the diamonds and cashing the ♣A, but why give up? If West has the ♣K, not too much to ask, you can make the hand by taking a simple finesse — but you have to take it now because this is the last time you are going to be in your hand. Yes, if the finesse loses, you go down three, but the chance of scoring up a game contract as opposed to losing an extra 100 points makes the finesse the winning action. Even vulnerable, you should go for it.

When entries are at a premium and the lead is in the weak hand, you may have to decide whether to take a simple or a repeatable finesse. Take the simple finesse; a repeatable finesse requires a return entry.

Yes, if East has the ♡AK and the ♣K you can make the hand by playing six rounds of diamonds, squeezing East to a pulp. But why play for miracles when a simple finesse sees you home? Besides, if East had all those cards, he might have doubled 1◇, intending to bid spades next.

BOTH VUL.		DEALER SOUTH	
West	**North**	**East**	**South**
			1♡
pass	1NT	pass	4♡
all pass			

North
♠ 5 3 2
♡ 4 3 2
◇ Q 4 2
♣ A 4 3 2

South (You)
♠ A Q 4
♡ A Q J 10 7 5
◇ K J 10
♣ 7

You open 1♡, partner correctly (in my view) responds 1NT rather than the more encouraging 2♡; you close proceedings with a leap to 4♡ and West leads the ♣K.

You win the ♣A, and realizing that this might well be the last time you will be in dummy, take the spade, not the heart, finesse. If the spade finesse works, you make the hand outright losing one spade, one heart, and one diamond. Meanwhile, even if the heart finesse works, East may have ♡Kxx, so you may still have a heart loser. What about the ◇Q as an entry? Perhaps, but if East has the ◇A, and is not a dear friend or a close relative, then he is not going to let you get to dummy with that ◇Q.

Milking a suit

Sometimes you will have only one 'communications suit' which allows you to travel from one hand to the other safely. The problem may be how to 'milk' this suit for the maximum number of entries.

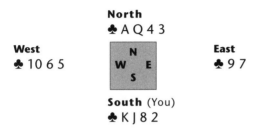

North
♣ A Q 4 3

West
♣ 10 6 5

East
♣ 9 7

South (You)
♣ K J 8 2

Say the lead is in your hand and you need to get to dummy three times in clubs. Can you do it? Yes. Cash the ♣K, and lead the ♣8 to the queen (one entry); later lead the ♣J to the ♣A (two entries) and finally the ♣2 to the ♣4 (three entries). (Interchange the ♣2 and ♣4 and you can't do it.)

More milking practice

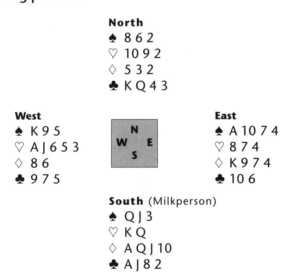

North
♠ 8 6 2
♡ 10 9 2
♢ 5 3 2
♣ K Q 4 3

West
♠ K 9 5
♡ A J 6 5 3
♢ 8 6
♣ 9 7 5

East
♠ A 10 7 4
♡ 8 7 4
♢ K 9 7 4
♣ 10 6

South (Milkperson)
♠ Q J 3
♡ K Q
♢ A Q J 10
♣ A J 8 2

You open 2NT, partner raises to 3NT and the ♡5 is led. You try the ♡10 hoping the jack appears, but no luck — the ♡4 (count) is played. It looks like East has three small hearts while West started with ♡AJxxx. Form a plan.

You have six sure tricks: four clubs, one diamond and the heart you have just taken. You need to develop three more diamond tricks. You must presume East has the ◇K. Even so, you are dealing with a repeatable finesse and may need as many as three dummy entries to pull this off. Cash the ♣A and lead the ♣8 to dummy's queen (one entry). Assuming both follow to the clubs so you know the suit is divided 3-2, take one diamond finesse, return to dummy with the ♣K overtaking your ♣J (two entries), and take a second diamond finesse, and finally, triumphantly, return to dummy's ♣4 using your carefully preserved ♣2 to take a third diamond finesse. Acknowledge the applause.

Another combination that can result in entry complications when misplayed is this (and similar positions):

North
Q 7 5

West
3

East
J 9 8 6

South (You)
A K 10 4 2

Whether the lead begins in your hand or dummy, start with a high honor from the two-honor side (your hand), then lead low to the one-honor side (dummy). If West shows out, you are in dummy to take the marked finesse. If you start with the queen and then lead low to the king or ace, even though you see West show out, you may not be able to get back to dummy to take the marked finesse.

The defining features of this combination find one hand with Qxx, Kxx or Axx and the facing hand with AK9x, AK10x, AK9xx, AK10xx, AQ9x, AQ10x, AQ9xx, AQ10xx, KQ9x, KQ10x, KQ9xx, or KQ10xx. For example, this position:

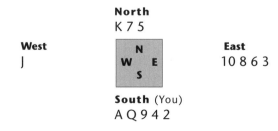

North
K 7 5

West
J

East
10 8 6 3

South (You)
A Q 9 4 2

Begin with the ace (two-honor side) and then lead low to the king (one-honor side). You are in dummy, and if West had a singleton ten or jack, you can now lead low to your nine, scooping up five tricks.

Unblocking

Unblocking a high honor when there is an equal honor in the facing hand is a painless way of creating an entry. What you have to determine early is which hand needs the entry.

However, if you *know* (perhaps you have counted out the distribution or East has bid the suit) that West started with a singleton or void, and there is a side-suit entry to dummy, lead low to the king and then low to the nine. This picks up J10xx in the East hand without the loss of a trick.

North
♠ Q 6
♡ K Q 9 8 6
◇ 4 2
♣ J 10 9 6

South (You)
♠ K J
♡ 4
◇ A K Q 5 3
♣ A Q 7 4 3

EAST-WEST VUL.		DEALER SOUTH	
West	**North**	**East**	**South**
			1◇
pass	1♡	pass	3♣
pass	4♣	pass	4♠
pass	5♣	all pass	

Against silent opposition you reach 5♣, with spades the unbid suit.

Scenario I: West leads the ♠A.

You have to lose two major suit aces so you must find the ♣K with East, but how are you going to get to dummy to take the club finesse? You could try ruffing a diamond, but you might get over-ruffed if East has the ♣K and a doubleton diamond. The simple solution is to unblock the ♠K at Trick 1, creating a dummy entry with the ♠Q.

Scenario II: West leads the ♠4.

East must have the ♠A so you play low from dummy and sure enough, East plays the ♠A. Dump the ♠K. Do it! The moral of the story? Be ever alert to get rid of an honor if an entry is needed to partner's hand and partner has an equal honor. Look at this example:

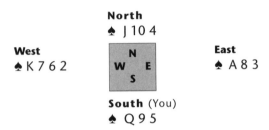

North
♠ J 10 4

West
♠ K 7 6 2

East
♠ A 8 3

South (You)
♠ Q 9 5

West leads the ♠2 and this is the layout of the spade suit. Say you desperately need to reach dummy with a spade to take a finesse in some other suit. If the contract is notrump, play the ♠10 in case West has underled the ♠AK. If East plays an honor, unblock the queen. Now, if West has the other high honor, as expected, you can lead up to the jack and forge a spade entry to dummy. At a suit contract, play low from dummy and unblock the queen when East takes the trick.

Strangely enough, if you need a spade entry to your hand, you should play the ♠10 from dummy. If East plays low (presumably at notrump), overtake and you have arrived in your hand. If East wins and returns a spade, play the nine. There is no way West can prevent you from taking this or the next spade trick in your hand. However, if you play low from dummy at Trick 1, West can keep you out of your hand by ducking the second spade if you play the nine, forcing dummy to take the trick. If you play the queen, he can win the second spade and now dummy must win the third round of the suit.

A little bravado is called for in our next example:

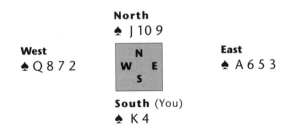

North
♠ J 10 9

West
♠ Q 8 7 2

East
♠ A 6 5 3

South (You)
♠ K 4

The contract is notrump and a low spade is led to East's ace. Since the best you can do is take one trick in this suit, unblock the king if you need a dummy entry. You still get a spade trick, but they can no longer play spades without letting you get to dummy. Make the same play if your spades are ♠Qx or ♠Qxx.

Probably the most common unblock occurs when declarer has honor doubleton facing a partner who has two honors.

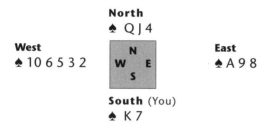

West leads low, dummy plays low, and if East plays the ♠A, unblock the ♠K liberating two spade winners in dummy. Of course, if it is more important to keep a hand entry than a dummy entry, play the ♠7 under the ace.

A slightly more complex example:

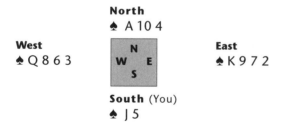

Either at a suit or notrump, West leads low, you play low from dummy, and East plays the king. Unblock the jack. Unblocking the jack allows you to lead low to the ten and take two spade tricks. If you don't unblock, the suit is blocked and you can be held to one trick if dummy has no other entry and West doesn't cover your jack. Also, if you started with Jxx, unblocking the jack affords you *two* spade entries to dummy.

Here's another unblock that many find hard to pull off at the table even when they sense it is the right play.

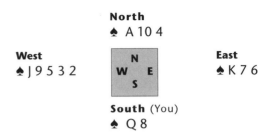

Again, either in a suit or notrump contract, dummy has no side-suit entries, and West leads low. You play low from dummy and East plays the king. Since the lead of a low card tends to show an honor, it is safe to assume that West has the jack; unblock the queen and later lead low to the ten to get your two spade tricks. What fun! How impressive!

That should make this last example a breeze for you:

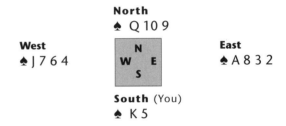

Again, either in a suit or notrump contract, West leads low; you play the nine from dummy and East the ace. Clearly East does not have the jack (he would have played it). It should be 100% safe to unblock the king and later lead low to the ten. Of course, if the dummy has an unassailable side-suit entry, no heroics are necessary.

Saving long suits from an ugly death

There is nothing more frustrating than having winning tricks in the dummy (or in your hand) and no way to use them because of entry problems. It is even more frustrating if you could have prevented this debacle by judiciously unblocking the suit as you play it. Often, this just needs a little foresight.

Frequently you find yourself playing a notrump contract where dummy presents you with a long, strong, minor suit with no outside entries. Careful! You may have to unblock *middle* spot cards from the short hand in order to run the suit.

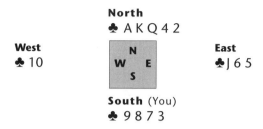

North
♣ A K Q 4 2

West   **East**
♣ 10   ♣ J 6 5

South (You)
♣ 9 8 7 3

It would be criminal not to be able to take five club tricks given this layout. But you have to unblock the 9-8-7 under the A-K-Q to pull it off. Then you can lead the ♣4 and underplay the ♣3, allowing the ♣2 to be the fifth trick. If you don't unblock, you get only four tricks.

This situation is similar, if you have no outside entries:

North
♣ A K 7 6 4 3

West   **East**
♣ Q 9   ♣ J 5

South (You)
♣ 10 8 2

If you need six club tricks, you must find a 2-2 club division. Even so, you must unblock the 10-8 under the A-K. If you don't, you bury three club tricks, taking only three tricks instead of six! If you only need five club tricks, lead the ♣10 and play low in dummy whatever West does, catering to a 3-1 division.

Middle-up-down

When it comes to making a lead, **middle-up-down** (MUD) refers to leading the middle card from three small. However, when it comes to the proper handling by declarer of a card combination it means something else entirely.

North
♠ A Q 9 2

South (You)
♠ K 10 7

Say you need four spade tricks and dummy has no outside entry. If the lead is in the short hand (the three cards), start with the middle card, in this case, the ♠10. If the lead is in the long hand, play a high honor, unblocking the ♠10. In either case the *middle* card from the short hand is played first, while a high honor is played from the long hand. Next, lead low from the long hand to the doubleton honor on the short side.

The short hand should always be on lead with the lowest card after two tricks have been played. It now looks like this:

North
♠ A 9

South (You)
♠ 7

When you lead the ♠7 and West follows small, you have the option of inserting the ♠9, catering to West having started with Jxxx, or playing the ♠A, catering to an original 3-3 split. It may be a guess or you may have a count, but the point is, you have a *choice*.

If you fail to unblock the ♠10 early, your last card will be the ♠10 instead of the ♠7, and the suit will be blocked. If there is no side dummy entry, you do not have a choice. You are forced to play the ace and hope for a 3-3 split.

If you start with the middle card from the short hand, when there is a lower or equal middle card in the facing hand, and then play the higher card from your hand next, you will double your options the third time the suit is played.

North
♠ Q J 8 3

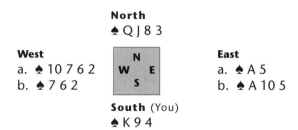

West
a. ♠ 10 7 6 2
b. ♠ 7 6 2

East
a. ♠ A 5
b. ♠ A 10 5

South (You)
♠ K 9 4

Conditions are ripe for a middle-up-down. Lead the ♠9 (see that ♠8 over there?) to the ♠Q (if the lead starts in dummy, play the queen and unblock the nine). Later cash the king, or lead low to the king, then the ♠4. Dummy will have the ♠J8 left. You have given yourself the option of inserting the ♠8, playing for West to have begun with 10xxx, or rising with the ♠J, playing for a 3-3 break. It's nice to have options, very nice.

Even eights are considered middle cards if the facing hand has the seven plus two honors!

North
♠ K Q 7 2

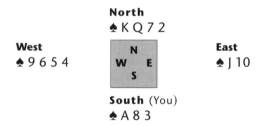

West
♠ 9 6 5 4

East
♠ J 10

South (You)
♠ A 8 3

Show some class and start by playing the ♠8 over to the ♠K (or, if the lead is in dummy, play the ♠K and unblock the ♠8, same difference). Next comes the ♠A. You have the ♠3 left and dummy has the ♠Q7. Since two high honors have dropped from the East hand, you have the option of inserting the ♠7, which would work given the diagram position. It is also the percentage play. However, if you find yourself left with the ♠8 instead of the ♠3, you have dug yourself an optionless grave.

The following middle-up-down plays don't quite fit the mold, but they are close enough.

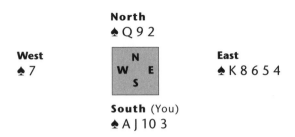

North
♠ Q 9 2

West
♠ 7

East
♠ K 8 6 5 4

South (You)
♠ A J 10 3

The lead is in dummy (for the last time) and you need four spade tricks. Lead the nine. Assuming East plays low, play the ♠3, then continue with the ♠Q. East has no answer.

Look what happens if you start with the ♠Q. If East covers, no problem; win the ace, cross to the nine, and so forth. But what if East plays low? The best you can do is play the ♠3 and repeat the finesse. Only this time you wind up in your hand, where you don't want to be because now you cannot repeat the proven finesse. Sad.

Play the same way with J9x facing AQ10x. Start with the nine and then the jack, and you'll find middle-up-down can save you a trick here too. Now look at this:

NEITHER VUL.   DEALER WEST

West	North	East	South
pass	pass	1◇	dbl
pass	1♡[1]	pass	7♣![2]
all pass			

1.   Partner has to bid something!
2.   You've gone stark-raving mad!

North
♠ Q 10 9
♡ 8 4 2
◇ 10 8 6 2
♣ J 3 2

West
♠ 8 6 2
♡ J 9 6 5
◇ Q 7 4 3
♣ 9 4

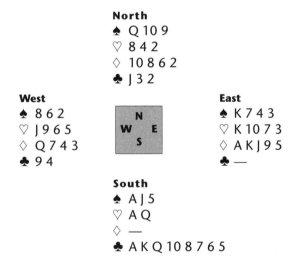

East
♠ K 7 4 3
♡ K 10 7 3
◇ A K J 9 5
♣ —

South
♠ A J 5
♡ A Q
◇ —
♣ A K Q 10 8 7 6 5

Playing matchpoints, you wind up in 7♣ after East opens the bidding 1◇. Being an optimist, you figure the heart finesse is going to work. Besides, a good partner will have something in spades, and perhaps a trump entry or two; perhaps you'll win the lottery as well. The opening lead is a diamond and sure enough partner has something in spades plus a trump entry to dummy. (Keep this partner.) Now the question is, can you take all the tricks, even if both major suit finesses work, having but one entry to dummy?

You can do it, but you must be familiar with this spade holding. Ruff the opening lead, draw two rounds of trumps, ending in dummy, and lead the ♠Q. If East obliges with a cover, your problems are over. You can reenter dummy in spades and take the heart finesse. But what if East doesn't cover? If you play low, leaving yourself with the ♠AJ, then if you repeat the spade finesse you wind up in your hand and can't take the heart finesse. If you take the heart finesse instead, you wind up in your hand and can't repeat the spade finesse. The answer is to unblock the ♠J under the ♠Q (key play), and continue with the ♠10. If East ducks again, you remain in dummy to take the heart finesse. If East covers, win the ace and enter dummy with the ♠9 to take the heart finesse.

A spectacular unblock

This last unblocking example is dedicated to bringing your partner to his feet and the opponents to their knees.

North
♠ —
♡ K 10 9 6 5
◇ K Q J 10
♣ A K 7 3

South
♠ A K Q J 10 9 8
♡ 7 4 3 2
◇ A
♣ 2

BOTH VUL.		DEALER SOUTH	
West	**North**	**East**	**South**
			1♠
pass	2♡	pass	3♠
pass	4♣	pass	4NT
pass	5◇	pass	6♠
pass	pass	dbl	all pass

You wind up in 6♠, which has been doubled by East for a heart lead, dummy's first bid suit. West leads the ♣Q, which tells you something about the heart suit — like West doesn't have any!

In any case, the club lead has removed the entry to dummy's diamonds, a blocked suit, but there is an answer. See it? Play the ♣AK, discarding the ◇A (applause) and then reel off as many diamonds as you can, discarding hearts. If each opponent has at least three diamonds, you make your doubled slam contract.

Overtaking

Another entry-conserving technique is the 'overtake'. You may overtake one honor with another or even one spot card with another spot card in order to wind up in the hand with the greater length, perhaps with the intent of developing a suit, perhaps for entry reasons. If executed properly, this technique can save you oodles of tricks.

NORTH-SOUTH VUL. DEALER NORTH

West	North	East	South
	1♣	pass	1NT
pass	3NT	all pass	

North
♠ 7 2
♡ K
◇ K 4 3
♣ A K Q J 9 8 3

```
    N
 W     E
    S
```

South (You)
♠ J 9 4 3
♡ A Q 5
◇ Q 10 6 5
♣ 7 4

Partner opens 1♣ and you decide to respond 1NT, preparing your apologies in advance if partner has four spades. Partner raises to 3NT and West leads the ♡J. Count your tricks!

There is every reason to overtake dummy's ♡K with your ace, cash the ♡Q, and then pour it on with seven more clubs. If you play low from your hand at Trick 1, you may not be able to get to your hand to use the ♡AQ. When you lead a diamond off dummy, the opponents may grab it and run off four spades. Now wouldn't that be lovely? Hands like this show you why you have to count tricks and look over the entire hand *before* playing to the first trick.

In our next example, partner, who has warned you that his pre-empts show thirteen cards, opens 3♣, but you try 3NT, anyway. West leads the ♠2 and partner actually tables a 'mountain' by his standards.

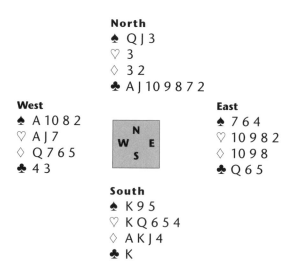

North
♠ Q J 3
♡ 3
♢ 3 2
♣ A J 10 9 8 7 2

West
♠ A 10 8 2
♡ A J 7
♢ Q 7 6 5
♣ 4 3

East
♠ 7 6 4
♡ 10 9 8 2
♢ 10 9 8
♣ Q 6 5

South
♠ K 9 5
♡ K Q 6 5 4
♢ A K J 4
♣ K

NORTH-SOUTH VUL. DEALER NORTH

West	North	East	South
	3♣	pass	3NT
all pass			

Clearly you have to bring in the clubs and dummy entries are at a premium. The answer is to win the first spade with the *king* (preserving the ♠QJ for a later entry), and overtake the ♣K to be able to continue the suit and drive out the queen. Upon winning the ♣Q, East can complicate your life by shifting to the ♡10. But if you cover and then win the third round of hearts before leading a spade, you survive. West, the player with the ♠A, has no more hearts.

Forcing an entry

There is yet another technique to force a dummy (or a hand) entry.

North
♣ 10 7 6

West
♣ 9 5 4

East
♣ Q 8 3

South (You)
♣ A K J 2

Say that it's a matter of life or death that you get to dummy and there are no entries. Try leading the ♣J. If East takes the trick, the ♣10 is an entry, if East ducks, he loses his club trick and you take four club tricks without loss.

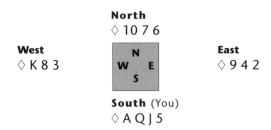

North
◇ 10 7 6

West
◇ K 8 3

East
◇ 9 4 2

South (You)
◇ A Q J 5

Another matter of life and death; you must get to dummy. Try the ◇Q. If West wins, you have your entry. If West ducks, try the ◇J. If West wins, you have your entry; if West ducks again, you take four diamond tricks.

Let's see how this idea plays out when everyone has thirteen cards.

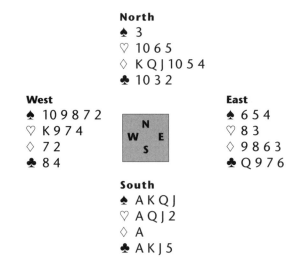

North
♠ 3
♡ 10 6 5
◇ K Q J 10 5 4
♣ 10 3 2

West
♠ 10 9 8 7 2
♡ K 9 7 4
◇ 7 2
♣ 8 4

East
♠ 6 5 4
♡ 8 3
◇ 9 8 6 3
♣ Q 9 7 6

South
♠ A K Q J
♡ A Q J 2
◇ A
♣ A K J 5

You wind up in 6NT — don't ask!

West leads the ♠10 and you think to yourself how nice it would be to get to those diamonds, but how? Say you play the ♡Q at Trick 2, hoping to smoke out the king. No luck, West senses your problem and ducks. Next you try the ♣J; no luck, East senses your problem and he also ducks. These guys are tough. Out of the woods you come with the ◊A followed by the ♡J. No luck, West ducks again. You can't seem to lose a trick, but on the other hand, you can't get to dummy.

Cash your top spades, your winning clubs, and the ♡A, leaving you with a small heart and a small club. If either hearts or clubs have divided 3-3, one of those little cards is a winner and you have twelve tricks. If neither suit breaks, as in the diagram, it's still not over. On this layout, you know that West has the high heart and a long spade and that East has a high club and a diamond. Exit with a club and take your contract-fulfilling trick when East has to lead a diamond to dummy. The last laugh is the sweetest.

Test yourself

Part 1 Suit management

1.

North (Dummy)
♠ A 4 2

South (You)
♠ K Q 8 7 5 3

a) Spades are trumps and you wish to draw two rounds ending in dummy, keeping entry flexibility in case the opponents' spades are divided 2-2. How should you do it?

b) How should you draw two rounds of trumps ending in your hand, keeping entry flexibility if spades are 2-2?

Solutions on page 45

2.

North (Dummy)
◇ K Q 4 2

South (You)
◇ A J 8 3

a) At notrump, the lead is in your hand, and you need to create three diamond entries to dummy (diamonds are 3-2). How do you do it?

b) At notrump, the lead is in dummy, and you need to create three diamond entries to your hand (diamonds are 3-2). How do you do it?

Solutions on page 45

3.

North (Dummy)
♣ A 10 9 8 3

South (You)
♣ K Q

a) At notrump, you have no side-suit entries to dummy, and you need five club tricks. How do you play the suit?
b) At notrump, one side-suit entry to dummy, and you need five club tricks. How do you play the suit?
c) At notrump, one side-suit entry to dummy, and you need four club tricks. How do you play the suit?

Solutions on page 45

4.

North (Dummy)
♡ K 10 9 8 7

South (You)
♡ Q

At notrump, you have two side-suit entries to dummy, and you need three heart tricks. How do you play the suit?

Solution on page 45

5.

North (Dummy)
♠ K 9 8 4 3

South (You)
♠ A Q

a) At notrump, with one side suit entry to dummy, and you need four spade tricks. How do you play the suit?
b) How do you play, given the same conditions, if you need five spade tricks?

Solutions on page 45

6.

North (Dummy)
♣ Q 9 7 2

South (You)
♣ A J 10 3

Solution on page 45

Clubs are trumps, you are in the dummy for the last time and you wish to draw trumps without losing a trick. How do you play the suit?

7.

North (Dummy)
◇ Q 10 3

South (You)
◇ A K 9 4 2

Solution on page 45

Diamonds are trumps, the lead is in dummy, and dummy has no side entries. How do you play the suit?

8.

North (Dummy)
♡ K J 8 3

South (You)
♡ Q 9 2

Solution on page 45

At notrump, dummy has no certain side entry, and you need three heart tricks. Furthermore, you suspect (hope) that East has Ax. How do you play the suit?

9.

North (Dummy)
♣ Q 10 9

South (You)
♣ A J 4

This is a side suit and the lead is in dummy. You not only wish to take, and possibly repeat, the club finesse, but you need to take a finesse in another suit as well. (You need both finesses to work to make your contract). The problem is that you cannot get back to dummy. How do you play clubs to take both finesses without losing a trick?

Solution on page 46

10.

North (Dummy)
◇ J 10 3

South (You)
◇ A K 9 4

You are playing notrump and West leads the ◇6. Assuming you need a *later* diamond entry to dummy, how do you manage the suit?

Solution on page 46

11.

North (Dummy)
♣ A K 7 6 4 3

South (You)
♣ 10 9 2

a) At notrump, dummy has no side-suit entries, and you need five club tricks. How do you play the suit?

b) How do you play the suit if you need all six tricks?

Solutions on page 46

Part 2 Play Hands

Hand 1

NEITHER VUL.		DEALER WEST	
West	**North**	**East**	**South**
1♢	pass	1♡	4♠
all pass			

Opening Lead: ♢K

North
♠ 6 4 3
♡ 5 2
♢ 7 6 5 3
♣ 7 6 3 2

South (You)
♠ K Q J 9 8 7 5
♡ A Q
♢ J 4
♣ A K

Solution on page 46

West begins by leading three top diamonds, East discarding a heart on the third diamond. Plan the play.

Hand 2

EAST-WEST VUL.		DEALER SOUTH	
West	**North**	**East**	**South**
			2NT
pass	3NT[1]	all pass	

1. Usually wiser not to use Stayman with 4-3-3-3 distribution.

Opening Lead: ♢K

North
♠ A 8 4 3
♡ 4 3 2
♢ J 6 5
♣ 7 4 3

South (You)
♠ K Q 10 2
♡ A Q J
♢ 9 7 4
♣ A K 8

Solution on page 47

The opponents reel off four diamond tricks, West ending up on lead. On the fourth diamond you discard a heart from dummy and a club from your hand, East discards a heart. West shifts to the ♣Q. How do you play from here?

Hand 3

North
♠ 5 4 3 2
♡ 5 3 2
◇ A J
♣ J 7 5 4

South
♠ A Q J
♡ A K Q J 9 8 4
◇ K 2
♣ 2

NORTH-SOUTH VUL.		DEALER: SOUTH	
West	**North**	**East**	**South**
			2♣[1]
pass	2◇[2]	pass	2♡
pass	3♡[3]	pass	4NT[4]
pass	5♣[5]	pass	6♡
all pass			

1. Strong and artificial.
2. Waiting.
3. Positive (should be a bit stronger).
4. RKB for ♡.
5. One keycard.

Opening lead: ♣K

West leads the ♣K and continues with the ♣A which you ruff. When you play a high heart at Trick 3, both follow. How do you continue? How will you play if one opponent shows out on the first round of hearts?

Solution on page 47

Hand 4

North
♠ J 6 4 3
♡ 9 7
◇ 9 8 4 2
♣ J 4 2

South
♠ A Q
♡ A K Q J 10 5 4
◇ K 3
♣ 9 6

EAST-WEST VUL.		DEALER NORTH	
West	**North**	**East**	**South**
	pass	1♣	4♡
pass	pass	dbl	all pass

Opening Lead: ♣5

East plays the queen, king, and ace of clubs, West following to the second round with the ♣7. Plan the play.

Solution on page 48

NORTH-SOUTH VUL. DEALER WEST

West	North	East	South
pass	1♣	pass	1♡
pass	2♡	pass	4♡
all pass			

Opening lead: ♠4

Hand 5

North
♠ K 6 3
♡ A 8 6 5
♢ K 2
♣ K 8 4 3

South (You)
♠ A 5 2
♡ Q J 10 9 4
♢ Q J 3
♣ Q 7

Solution on page 49

Plan the play.

BOTH VUL.   DEALER EAST

West	North	East	South
		3♢	6♠
all pass			

Opening lead: ♢4

Hand 6

North
♠ 8 5
♡ J 10 7
♢ 10 8 2
♣ A K 8 5 2

South (You)
♠ A K Q J 7 6 4 2
♡ A K 6
♢ A 3
♣ —

Solution on page 50

East deals and opens 3♢; you control yourself and only overcall 6♠! Everybody passes. West leads his singleton diamond and you win the first trick with the ace. You play the ♠A and East discards a diamond. You have a heart loser and a diamond loser, but you do have the alluring ♣AK over there — but no apparent way to get to them. Believe it or not, there is a way. Can you find it?

Test yourself — solutions

Part 1

1. a) Play the ♠K and then a middle spade to the ace. Dummy remains with the ♠4 and you have the ♠3 to get over there again if need be.

b) Play the ace, retaining the ♠3, and then the ♠2 over to the king. Entry flexibility is maintained.

2. a) Play the ◇A and then the ◇8 to the ◇Q, later the ◇J to the ◇K, and finally, the ◇3 to the ◇4.

b) Play the ◇K, then the ◇4 to the ◇J, later the ◇Q to the ◇A, and finally the ◇2 to the ◇8.

Note: If diamonds break 4-1, you cannot manage three entries to either hand, but playing as directed, at least you will take four diamond tricks.

3. a) Play the ♣K, and then overtake the ♣Q, hoping one opponent has ♣Jx.

b) Play the ♣KQ, cross to dummy, and play the ♣A.

c) Play the ♣K, overtake the ♣Q and drive out the ♣J. You still have an entry to get over there to use the two established clubs (if the ♣J has not dropped singleton or doubleton).

4. Play the queen and overtake to drive out the ace. Next, use one side-suit entry to play the ten to drive out the jack. Later use your last entry to cash your three remaining tricks. If you don't overtake the queen, a crafty opponent may allow you to hold the trick, and you will be short a dummy entry to set up the suit.

5. a) Play the ace and overtake the queen. If either opponent has a ♠10x or ♠Jx, you can drive out the remaining honor with dummy's nine and establish four tricks. If no honor drops after the first two plays, lead low and hope for a 3-3 division.

b) Play the ace and queen and enter dummy to play the king. You need a 3-3 division or someone holding ♠J10 doubleton.

6. Run the nine, playing the three under it. If that holds, lead the queen. This is better than leading the queen immediately which East, holding four clubs, might not cover.

7. Lead the ten to the king, then low to the queen. If West shows out on the second round, lead low for a finesse of the nine. (Middle-up-down.)

8. Lead the nine to the king if the lead is in the closed hand or lead the king and underplay the nine from your hand if the lead is in the dummy; then low to the queen and finally low to the eight assuming you think (or know) East has a doubleton.

9. Play the queen and if it is not covered, underplay the jack and lead the ten. If this is covered, win and return to the ♣9 for your other finesse. If the ten is not covered, you remain in dummy to take the other finesse.

10. Win the first trick in your hand with the king (or ace) to ensure a later entry to dummy by leading low toward the J-10. If you win the first trick cheaply in either hand, you will not be able to get to dummy later in diamonds.

11. a) Lead the ♣10 and if it is covered, win the king and then lead low to the nine. If the ten is not covered, play low. You are willing to concede one club to get five in return; the suit may break 3-1.

    b) This time you need a 2-2 break, so play the king-ace, but be sure to unblock the nine and ten to 'liberate' the suit. If you don't, the suit will be blocked even with a 2-2 division.

Part 2

Hand 1

NEITHER VUL.   DEALER WEST

West	North	East	South
1◇	pass	1♡	4♠
all pass			

Trick 1: ◇K ◇3 ◇8 ◇4
Trick 2: ◇A ◇5 ◇2 ◇J
Trick 3: ◇Q ◇6 ♡6 ?

North
♠ 6 4 3
♡ 5 2
◇ 7 6 5 3
♣ 7 6 3 2

West
♠ A 10
♡ 7 4 3
◇ A K Q 10 9
♣ J 10 8

East
♠ 2
♡ K J 10 9 8 6
◇ 8 2
♣ Q 9 5 4

South (You)
♠ K Q J 9 8 7 5
♡ A Q
◇ J 4
♣ A K

TIP

With a powerful trump suit and trump entries at a premium, save the small trumps in the long trump hand in case something good develops.

Don't tell me you ruffed the third diamond with the ♠5, just don't tell me. If you did, you can no longer make the hand. You need the ♠5 to get to the ♠6 in order to take the heart finesse (assuming a 2-1 spade break, of course).

Hand 2

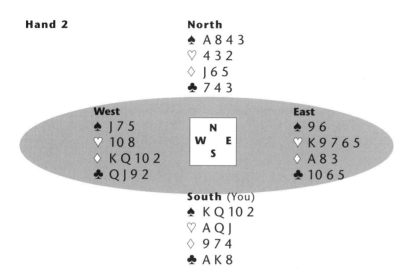

North
- ♠ A 8 4 3
- ♡ 4 3 2
- ◇ J 6 5
- ♣ 7 4 3

West
- ♠ J 7 5
- ♡ 10 8
- ◇ K Q 10 2
- ♣ Q J 9 2

East
- ♠ 9 6
- ♡ K 9 7 6 5
- ◇ A 8 3
- ♣ 10 6 5

South (You)
- ♠ K Q 10 2
- ♡ A Q J
- ◇ 9 7 4
- ♣ A K 8

EAST-WEST VUL.   DEALER SOUTH

West	North	East	South
			2NT
pass	3NT[1]	all pass	

1. Usually wiser not to use Stayman with 4-3-3-3 distribution.

Opening Lead: ◇K

Trick 1: ◇K ◇5 ◇8 ◇4
Trick 2: ◇2 ◇6 ◇A ◇7
Trick 3: ◇3 ◇9 ◇Q ◇J
Trick 4: ◇2 ♡2 ♡5 ♣8
Trick 5: ♣Q ?

You have to play East for the ♡K, and you figure to need two dummy entries to repeat the heart finesse. Spades is the only suit that offers entry possibilities. Start with the ♠KQ, and assuming both follow (you will almost certainly need spades to be 3-2 to make the contract), lead the ♠10 to the ♠A (entry #1) to take the first heart finesse. Assuming that works, enter dummy with the ♠8, using your carefully preserved ♠2 (entry #2), and repeat the heart finesse. Making three notrump. Notice that a contract of 4♠ on the 4-4 fit has no play as you must lose three diamonds and a club.

Tip

When entries to dummy are scarce, and your communications suit is equally divided between your hand and dummy, conserve your lowest card (♠2) as your final entry card to the facing hand.

Hand 3

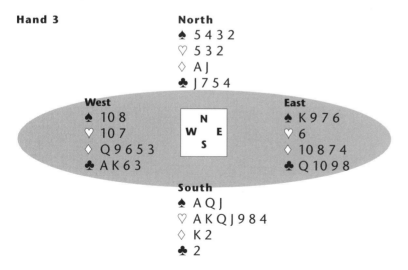

North
- ♠ 5 4 3 2
- ♡ 5 3 2
- ◇ A J
- ♣ J 7 5 4

West
- ♠ 10 8
- ♡ 10 7
- ◇ Q 9 6 5 3
- ♣ A K 6 3

East
- ♠ K 9 7 6
- ♡ 6
- ◇ 10 8 7 4
- ♣ Q 10 9 8

South
- ♠ A Q J
- ♡ A K Q J 9 8 4
- ◇ K 2
- ♣ 2

NORTH-SOUTH VUL.   DEALER SOUTH

West	North	East	South
			2♣[1]
pass	2◇[2]	pass	2♡
pass	3♡[3]	pass	4NT[4]
pass	5♣[5]	pass	6♡
all pass			

1. Strong and artificial.
2. Waiting.
3. Positive (should be a bit stronger)
4. RKB for ♡.
5. One.

Trick 1: ♣K ♣4 ♣10 ♣2
Trick 2: ♣A ♣5 ♣8 ?

It's a given that you ruffed the second club with something other than the ♡4! I won't even insult you by asking. After you ruff and play a high trump, you have verified the trump position. If hearts are 2-1, draw a second trump, and use the ♡5 and the ◇A as your dummy entries to take two spade finesses. You are assuming, of course, that the ♠K is with East.

If trumps are 3-0, you can't get to dummy with a trump, so you have to lead your low diamond to the jack, hoping to get to dummy twice to take two spade finesses. Courage. You are hoping West has the ◇Q and doesn't scuttle your plans by playing the queen (leaving you only one diamond entry). If West does play the queen, hold your hand back.

EAST-WEST VUL.   DEALER NORTH

West	North	East	South
	pass	1♣	4♡
pass	pass	dbl	all pass

Trick 1: ♣5 ♣2 ♣Q ♣6
Trick 2: ♣K ♣9 ♣7 ♣4
Trick 3: ♣A ?

Hand 4

North
♠ J 6 4 3
♡ 9 7
◇ 9 8 4 2
♣ J 4 2

West
♠ 9 5 2
♡ 8 6 2
◇ J 7 6 5
♣ 10 7 5

East
♠ K 10 8 7
♡ 3
◇ A Q 10
♣ A K Q 8 3

South
♠ A Q
♡ A K Q J 10 5 4
◇ K 3
♣ 9 6

When you need an extra dummy entry, do not be afraid to take a seemingly unnecessary finesse to get there. It isn't unnecessary if you have to get there an extra time, it's vital.

Ruff the third club high, and lead a heart to the seven! You need two dummy entries: one to lead up to the ◇K and one to take the spade finesse; both the ◇A and the ♠K are probably located with East on the bidding. If West has the ♡8 you are the hero of the moment. If East has it, don't call and don't write.

Hand 5

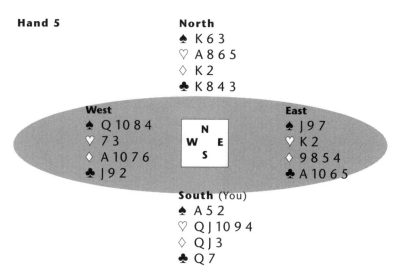

North
♠ K 6 3
♡ A 8 6 5
◇ K 2
♣ K 8 4 3

West
♠ Q 10 8 4
♥ 7 3
◇ A 10 7 6
♣ J 9 2

East
♠ J 9 7
♥ K 2
◇ 9 8 5 4
♣ A 10 6 5

South (You)
♠ A 5 2
♡ Q J 10 9 4
◇ Q J 3
♣ Q 7

NORTH-SOUTH VUL. DEALER WEST

West	North	East	South
pass	1♣	pass	1♡
pass	2♡	pass	4♡
all pass			

Opening lead: ♠4

Time and entries are the keys to this problem. You are faced with a possible loser in each suit, but you can dispose of dummy's spade loser on a diamond if you do it quickly — before your remaining spade stopper is removed. You don't have time to take the heart finesse. If it loses and a spade comes back, your extra diamond winner will have to wait until the next hand; it's not going to be good for anything on this one.

No, you must play diamonds before hearts. There is another problem, however: if the opponents win the second round of diamonds, not the first, you must have a way back to your hand to cash a third diamond after they drive out your remaining spade stopper. The answer is to win the ♠K in dummy at Trick 1 and then play the ◇K. Even if they win the second diamond and continue with a spade, you win in your hand and can discard dummy's remaining spade on a high diamond. Now you can take the heart finesse.

When setting up a side suit for discards takes precedence over drawing trumps, make provisions for a convenient return entry to the suit that you are establishing.

BOTH VUL.   DEALER EAST

West	North	East	South
		3◇	6♠
all pass			

Trick 1: ◇4 ◇2 ◇5 ◇A

Hand 6

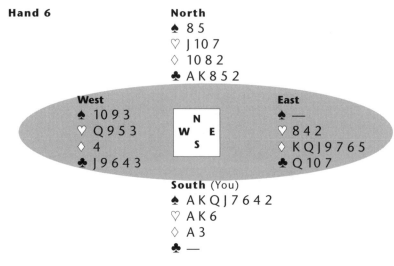

North
♠ 8 5
♡ J 10 7
◇ 10 8 2
♣ A K 8 5 2

West
♠ 10 9 3
♡ Q 9 5 3
◇ 4
♣ J 9 6 4 3

East
♠ —
♡ 8 4 2
◇ K Q J 9 7 6 5
♣ Q 10 7

South (You)
♠ A K Q J 7 6 4 2
♡ A K 6
◇ A 3
♣ —

Play the ace, king, and deuce of spades at Tricks 2, 3 and 4. West must win the trick and either lead a club or lead away from the ♡Q. Either way you are in dummy. You were told at the beginning of the chapter that deuces were the best cards in your hand, and this deal goes a long way toward proving it!

Key ideas from Chapter 1.

- **Entry management** is the key to almost every hand you play.
- Do not play too quickly to the first trick (this advice holds true for any lesson); most planning, particularly entry planning, is done at this time.
- It is important to keep low cards in your long, strong suits for entry purposes. When holding a long, powerful trump suit, check dummy's trumps before ruffing low. You might need that trump to enter dummy later in the hand.
- When drawing trumps, if you can leave trump in both hands, make sure you remain with **trump entry flexibility**. Translation: that you can get to dummy by leading a trump from your hand and you can get to your hand by leading a trump from dummy. Do not block the trump suit.
- Unblocking with a doubleton honor when the facing hand has two honors and no side-suit entries is a common entry-saving play (for example, with Kx facing QJx).
- Overtaking a singleton honor with another honor is an **entry-conserving play** — if the spot cards justify the overtake.
- There will be times when you may have to take a finesse in a suit in which you have no losers in order to create an extra entry.
- When you can win a trick in either hand, ask yourself where you will need the entry most.
- **Middle Up Down** is a way of referring to the best way to handle card combinations such as the K92 facing the AQ83. Notice that the long hand holding the AQ83 has the 8, an equal, but lower, intermediate than the short hand which holds the K92. It is important to start with the 9, the middle card from the short side, or play an honor from the long side and unblock the 9 from the short side. The second play is the honor from the short side, in this case the king. This leaves the lead in the short hand with the deuce facing the Q8 (or A8). Declarer now has the option of leading low to the 8.

Tricks on the Side

They also serve who only stand and wait.

JOHN MILTON

The key to making many trump contracts (or notrump contracts for that matter) is working with dummy's long suit with the eventual goal of making the small cards winners in order to discard losers from your hand. In order to pull this off, certain ingredients have to be in place:

1. Declarer (you) has losers that you must get rid of if you are to make your contract.
2. Dummy's suit must be long enough that it can be established for some long-card winners.
3. You must have enough trumps in your hand to be able to ruff two or three (or more!) times in the closed hand and still be able to draw trumps.
4. You must have enough dummy entries (and you thought that you were through with entries) both to establish the long suit and then to get back over there to use it. Without enough entries, you are spinning your wheels.
5. You must be able to draw trumps before cashing the established winners in dummy.

Basic technique

Any five-card suit can be established if there are enough dummy entries and the opponents' cards break in a civilized manner.

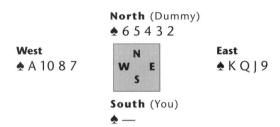

North (Dummy)
♠ 6 5 4 3 2

West
♠ A 10 8 7

East
♠ K Q J 9

South (You)
♠ —

Assume hearts are trumps, you have to get rid of a loser, and the only place it can go is on one of dummy's spades! (Let's hope you don't get into contracts like this very often.) If you have enough trumps in your hand and enough entries to dummy, you can actually set up one of those spades if the opponents each have four spades. However, you need five, count 'em, five dummy entries to do it — four times to get over there to trump spades and one more entry to get back there to use the established spade. Of course you must be able to draw trumps before you can cash that fifth spade. Would you like to see the entire hand? Here it is:

BOTH VUL.		DEALER SOUTH	
West	**North**	**East**	**South**
			4♡
pass	4♠[1]	pass	5♠[2]
pass	7♡	all pass	

1. Asking bid.
2. 5th step response = void.

You're Kidding

North
♠ 6 5 4 3 2
♡ Q 2
♢ A K 4
♣ A K 3

West
♠ K J 10 8
♡ 9 5
♢ Q 9 8 2
♣ Q J 10

East
♠ A Q 9 7
♡ 4
♢ J 10 7 6
♣ 9 7 6 4

South (You)
♠ —
♡ A K J 10 8 7 6 3
♢ 5 3
♣ 8 5 2

After you open 4♡ and show a void in response to partner's 4♠ asking bid, partner slams you into 7♡! West leads the ♣Q and there you are.

Your main hope is to set up dummy's fifth spade and you do have the five dummy entries you need — providing you start right in. Ruff a spade; ace of hearts and a heart to dummy, which removes the enemy trumps. Ruff a spade; back to a club; ruff a spade; over to a diamond; ruff a spade and what do you know, they are 4-4! Back to dummy with a diamond and discard that miserable club loser on dummy's fifth spade.

Take heart. Dummy's long suit is not always going to be that anemic. Let's try something that looks a little more down-to-earth.

> When establishing a side suit, if you are fortunate to have both side suit and trump entries to dummy, use the trump entries first.

Subtracting your way
to stardom

North
- ♠ 10 8 4
- ♡ K 10 3
- ◇ K 9 7 6 4
- ♣ A 2

West
- ♠ 5 2
- ♡ 9 7
- ◇ Q 10 8 3
- ♣ J 10 7 6 5

East
- ♠ A K 9 7 6
- ♡ 6 5
- ◇ J 5
- ♣ K Q 9 8

South (You)
- ♠ Q J 3
- ♡ A Q J 8 4 2
- ◇ A 2
- ♣ 4 3

NORTH-SOUTH VUL. DEALER SOUTH

West	North	East	South
			1♡
pass	2◇	2♠	3♡
pass	4♡	all pass	

Opening lead: ♠5

The opponents waste no time taking the first three tricks, West ruffing the third round of spades. When West shifts to a club, taken by dummy's ace, you have your work cut out for you. You must establish at least one of dummy's diamonds for a club pitch.

The general rule is to attack the long suit early. Just do it! Cross to the ◇A and then back to the ◇K, to start work on setting up the diamonds.

When establishing dummy's suit, count the suit as it is being played to know how many more cards the opponents have in the suit and when the remaining cards in the suit are winners.

> When setting up a long suit, if the only entries to dummy are in the trump suit, don't squander them; coordinate them with your long suit establishment. In other words, don't draw trumps prematurely if you need the trumps in dummy for entries!

Personally, I find the subtraction method works pretty well. It goes like this. First determine how many cards the opponents have in dummy's long suit. In this case, six. Each time the suit is played

The subtraction method can be used not only when establishing dummy's long suit, but also when drawing trumps. For example, on this hand when dummy tables you see that the opponents have four hearts. After West trumps your spade winner, they have three. When you cross to dummy with the ♡10 and both follow, they have one left. It works; it's easy.

and both opponents follow, subtract two from that number. When you play a diamond to the ace, they have four diamonds left; when you cross back to the king, they have two left. When you trump a third diamond from dummy, East discards and West follows. They have one diamond left. No sweat. Cross to the ♡10; ruff another diamond (now they have none left), return to the king of hearts and discard your losing club on dummy's fifth diamond.

Frequently you will find yourself working with side suits having a total of seven cards between your hand and dummy. Be forewarned that their cards are much more likely to divide 4-2 (48%) than 3-3 (36%). Of course if they divide 5-1, it just wasn't your day.

Frequently the long suit you have to work with will have a loser or two. It's more a matter of dummy entries and a strong trump suit than how pathetic the long suit looks. Just remember you have to give in order to receive. Watch.

EAST-WEST VUL.		DEALER SOUTH	
South	**West**	**North**	**East**
1♡	1♠	2♡	3♠¹
4♡	all pass		

1.   Preemptive.

Opening lead: ♠K

Talk about anemic suits

North
♠ J 8
♡ K 10 6
♢ 9 8 5 3 2
♣ K 8 6

West
♠ K Q 10 7 5
♡ 5 3 2
♢ A Q
♣ J 10 7

East
♠ 9 6 4 3
♡ 7
♢ K J 10 6
♣ Q 9 5 2

South (You)
♠ A 2
♡ A Q J 9 8 4
♢ 7 4
♣ A 4 3

You have four losers: a spade (after you win the ♠A), two diamonds, and a 'slow' club. One too many. Look to the length in dummy before throwing up your hands in despair.

Dummy has a five-card diamond suit. True, it is a rather pathetic five-card suit; but you've already seen how pathetic suits can be set up. Dummy has the entries, your side has a long, strong trump suit, and you have a loser(s) you have to get rid of; don't waste time. Start establishing the long suit *early*.

Win the ♠A and lead a diamond. West wins (they have four diamonds left, remember?), cashes a spade, and exits with the ♣J, a
strong defense. You win in your hand (conserving the ♣K as a later
dummy entry), and concede a second diamond. West wins (now
they have two diamonds left) and plays a second club. The race is
on! You win the ♣K and ruff a diamond high, West showing out.
Now they have one diamond left.

Cross to dummy with the ♡10 (now they have two hearts left) and
ruff a diamond high, establishing dummy's fifth diamond. It's not
over yet! They have two trumps left and you have to draw all of
their trumps *ending in dummy*. So play a high heart and then a low
one to dummy's king; then, finally, you can play your established
diamond and discard your losing club.

When the only entries to dummy
are in the trump suit, arrange to
draw trumps **ending** in dummy
after you have established winners in dummy. A biggie.

North (Dummy)
♠ 3 2
♡ A 4 3

West
♡ J 6 5

East
♡ 10 2

South (You)
♡ K Q 9 8

Pretend hearts are trumps and the two little spades in dummy are
both winners (you've set them up as only you can) having trumped
one with the ♡7 (in case you're wondering where it is). If there are
no side entries to dummy other than the ♡A, you must draw
trumps ending in dummy. Play the king, the queen, then low to
the ace.

It stands to reason that the longer the suit in the dummy, the easier
it is to establish; no good player ever takes his eye off anything
resembling a possibly usable six-card side suit in the dummy.

When establishing dummy's long
suit while holding a number of
high trumps, be sure to trump
high and not risk getting over-
ruffed with a nondescript spot
card.

NORTH-SOUTH VUL. DEALER SOUTH

West	North	East	South
			1♠
pass	2♣	pass	3♡
pass	3♠	pass	4♣
pass	4◇	pass	4NT[1]
pass	5♣[2]	pass	6♠
all pass			

1. RKCB 1430 Responses
2. One.

Opening lead: ◇Q

Using Dummy's Jewels

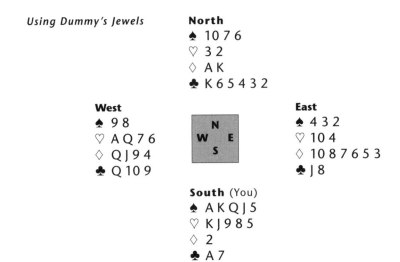

North
♠ 10 7 6
♡ 3 2
◇ A K
♣ K 6 5 4 3 2

West
♠ 9 8
♡ A Q 7 6
◇ Q J 9 4
♣ Q 10 9

East
♠ 4 3 2
♡ 10 4
◇ 10 8 7 6 5 3
♣ J 8

South (You)
♠ A K Q J 5
♡ K J 9 8 5
◇ 2
♣ A 7

The idea is to avoid the heart guess (it may not be guessable, as in the diagram!) by establishing the clubs. However, the only entry to dummy outside of clubs after the diamond lead is the ♠10. So not only do you have to conserve the ♠10 over there, but you must plan to draw trumps ending in dummy after the clubs are established. Let's get to work!

Lead a club to the ace (they have three left), a club to the king (they have one left), and trump a club high (they don't have any more clubs and you have three winning clubs in dummy). Play two high spades and then cross to dummy's ♠10 and discard four of your five hearts; three go on the clubs and one on the ◇K.

Again, in this example, there were no entries to dummy outside of the trump suit. Given these conditions, if you can't draw trumps ending in dummy — forget it, you are spinning your wheels. Look at this next deal:

Don't Spin Your Wheels

North (Dummy)
♠ J 8 2
♡ Q J
◇ A K 7 4 3
♣ 4 3 2

```
      N
  W       E
      S
```

South (You)
♠ 10 9 6
♡ A K 10 9 7 3
◇ J 2
♣ A J

| BOTH VUL. | | DEALER SOUTH | |
West	**North**	**East**	**South**
			1♡
pass	2◇	pass	2♡
pass	3♡	pass	4♡
all pass			

Opening lead: ♠A
(Ace from AKx(x) at Trick 1 only)

West continues with the spade king and a third spade to East's queen. East shifts to the ♣K. What is to become of your club loser? You cannot possibly set up dummy's diamonds no matter how evenly they divide. The reason is that the only entries to the dummy are in the trump suit and you cannot draw all of their trumps ending in dummy after setting up the diamonds. Forget diamonds.

Instead, win the ♣A and play all six of your hearts, reducing all hands to three cards. If you get lucky, the player with the ♣Q (surely East) will have been dealt four diamonds or will err on the discards. In the first case, East is simply squeezed between clubs and diamonds. In the second, East may think he is getting squeezed and discard the ♣Q in order to hold on to ◇Qxx — which would be correct if you had started with a singleton ♣A and three diamonds. Opponents make mistakes when discarding on long suits, or haven't you noticed?

When the only entries to dummy's long suit are trump entries and you cannot possibly draw trump ending in dummy, you cannot set up a long suit by ruffing. Try something else.

When you are short of entries, look for ways to make the most of them. The technique of ducking a trick in dummy's long suit is a common entry-saving play.

If you have all the tricks but one, no long suit that can be set up, no possibility of ruffing a loser in dummy, play each and every one of your trumps and hope something good happens — like an errant discard or a bona fide squeeze.

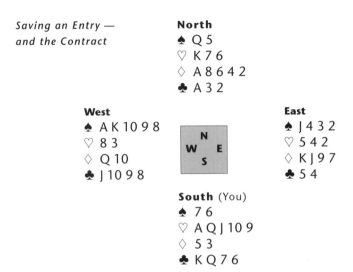

BOTH VUL.		DEALER SOUTH	
West	**North**	**East**	**South**
			1♡
1♠	2♢	2♠	pass
pass	4♡	all pass	

Opening lead: ♠K
(King from AKx(x) in supported suits; Ace from AKx(x) in unsupported suits)

Saving an Entry — and the Contract

North
♠ Q 5
♡ K 7 6
♢ A 8 6 4 2
♣ A 3 2

West
♠ A K 10 9 8
♡ 8 3
♢ Q 10
♣ J 10 9 8

East
♠ J 4 3 2
♡ 5 4 2
♢ K J 9 7
♣ 5 4

South (You)
♠ 7 6
♡ A Q J 10 9
♢ 5 3
♣ K Q 7 6

Say that West cashes two spades and shifts to the ♣J. You are staring at a certain diamond loser and a possible club loser. (Clubs may break 3-3 for everybody else, but for you they always break 4-2 or worse!) Therefore your plan should be to work with dummy's diamonds to set up at least one diamond for a possible club discard. However, there is a big difference between playing the ace of diamonds and another diamond and ducking a diamond the first time and then playing the ace.

The difference is one entry! Say the diamonds are 4-2 as expected. If you play the ace and another diamond, you are going to have to get to dummy three more times to set up the long diamond: twice to ruff diamonds, once to use the established diamond. The trouble is, there are only two entries to dummy after the ace of diamonds has been played.

Holding xx in your hand facing Axxxx(x) in dummy, it is almost always (there are no 'always' in bridge, but this one is close to it) right to duck the first round of the suit and then play the ace and trump one. It saves a dummy entry.

However, if you duck a diamond and then lead a diamond to the ace and ruff a diamond, you will only need two more dummy entries to establish the suit. Therefore your play is to win the club shift in your hand and *duck* a diamond. Win the club return in your hand, saving the ♣A in dummy for a later entry, and play a diamond to the ace and ruff a diamond (necessarily) high. Then play three rounds of hearts ending in dummy. Now you can ruff a second diamond, establishing dummy's fifth diamond. The ♣A is just sitting over there waiting for you to come to dummy and cash dummy's fifth diamond.

When setting up dummy's long suit, use the trump entries first and the side suit entries last. This is a recording.

Setting up a long suit in dummy by ruffing requires dummy entries. Sometimes, as we saw in the previous chapter, you may have to take a seemingly unnecessary finesse in order to create an extra dummy entry.

North
♠ J 9

South (You)
♠ A K Q 4 3 2

Here spades are trumps and you need two dummy entries in spades. What you have to do is lead low to the nine and close your eyes. With luck, when you open them you won't see East's ♠10 on the table.

Don't play Scrooge with dummy entries. What does that mean? It means that when you are establishing a suit, and your only entries to dummy are in the trump suit, you may have to ruff high in your hand in order to save a lower trump to eventually get to dummy.

North (Dummy)
♠ A 10 3

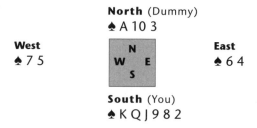

West
♠ 7 5

East
♠ 6 4

South (You)
♠ K Q J 9 8 2

Spades are trumps and you may have to get to dummy three times in the spade suit: twice to ruff the suit you are establishing, and once more to use it. Translation: you can enter dummy with the ♠10 and the ♠A, but in order to enter dummy with the ♠3, you must preserve the ♠2. *Save that deuce!* Nothing impresses partner more than seeing you get to dummy by using a deuce to get to a three.

As we saw in the last chapter, entry management requires planning. Sometimes you have to look ahead before deciding on your exact line of play.

Keeping your Eye on the Ball

North
♠ Q 2
♡ K 3 2
◊ A Q 6 5 3
♣ 10 9 2

```
      N
   W     E
      S
```

South (You)
♠ A K J 10 9 3
♡ A J 7
◊ 8 4
♣ 7 6

You worm your way into 4♠ and West leads the king of clubs. This is followed by the queen of clubs and a third club to East's ace, which you ruff. In an effort to get rid of a possible heart loser, you take the diamond finesse. It is a good rule of thumb to remember that nine times out of ten you will be attacking a suit that is unevenly divided between your hand and dummy (either to set it up if dummy's suit is longer or to ruff it in dummy if your suit is longer). Evenly divided suits (hearts) with possible 'slow' losers are the pits and are seldom played early.

Alas, the diamond finesse loses and a heart comes back. Do not take your eye off the ball now! Your plan is to set up those diamonds and you will need that ♡K as a vital return entry to dummy once the diamonds are established! Win the ♡A, cross to the ◊A and ruff a diamond, merrily counting those diamonds. If diamonds are 3-3, draw trumps, enter dummy with the ♡K, and claim. If diamonds are 4-2 (the expected 4-2), return to dummy with the ♠Q and ruff a second diamond, establishing dummy's fifth diamond. Now draw trumps and enter dummy with that carefully preserved ♡K to cash the fifth diamond.

Attack unevenly divided suits before evenly divided ones.

If the opponents have the nerve to attack a dummy entry and you have a choice of winning the trick in your hand or in the dummy, and you need later entries to the dummy, guess where you should win the trick.

Practice hands

Hand 1 *Make partner proud*

NEITHER VUL.   DEALER SOUTH

West	North	East	South
			3♡
pass	4♡	all pass	

Opening Lead: ◇K

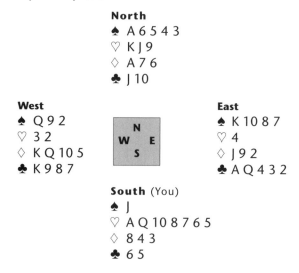

North
♠ A 6 5 4 3
♡ K J 9
◇ A 7 6
♣ J 10

West
♠ Q 9 2
♡ 3 2
◇ K Q 10 5
♣ K 9 8 7

East
♠ K 10 8 7
♡ 4
◇ J 9 2
♣ A Q 4 3 2

South (You)
♠ J
♡ A Q 10 8 7 6 5
◇ 8 4 3
♣ 6 5

Once the ◇A is played from dummy, you have four quick minor suit losers and the only place to park one of them is on dummy's fifth spade. Translation: you need to find their spades divided 4-3. It also means you have to trump three spades in your own hand and get back to dummy to use the fifth spade. Count entries.

After you play the ♠A and trump a spade, you must get back to dummy two more times to trump two more spades and then a third time to use the established spade. This requires three dummy entries outside of the ♠A. Do you have them? Yes. You have three trump entries, but you mustn't squander them prematurely.

Win the ◇A, and play the ♠A and ruff a spade; enter dummy with the ♡9 and trump another spade. Travel back to dummy with the ♡J and trump a third spade, establishing dummy's fifth spade. Now triumphantly return to dummy with the ♡K to enjoy the fruits of your labor, dummy's lowly ♠6, your tenth trick.

Key point
- When the only entries to dummy are in the trump suit, do not squander those entries by drawing trumps prematurely. Those entries are needed for communications.

NEITHER VUL.		DEALER SOUTH	
West	**North**	**East**	**South**
			2♣
pass	2♡	pass	2♠
pass	3♣	pass	3♠
pass	4♠	pass	4NT[1]
pass	5♣	pass	5NT
pass	6♡	pass	7♠[2]
all pass			

1. Simple Blackwood.
2. Although you can only count twelve top tricks, there should be many chances to bag a thirteenth.

Opening lead: ◊10

Hand 2 *You only get hands like this in books*

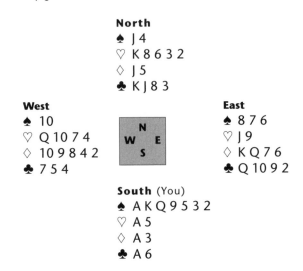

North
♠ J 4
♡ K 8 6 3 2
◊ J 5
♣ K J 8 3

West
♠ 10
♡ Q 10 7 4
◊ 10 9 8 4 2
♣ 7 5 4

East
♠ 8 7 6
♡ J 9
◊ K Q 7 6
♣ Q 10 9 2

South (You)
♠ A K Q 9 5 3 2
♡ A 5
◊ A 3
♣ A 6

Your plan is to establish dummy's fifth heart for a diamond discard. For this to work, you need hearts to be no worse than 4-2 (almost 85%) which is far better odds than taking a club finesse or trying to ruff out the ♣Q. As ever, entry management must enter into your planning.

In order to set up dummy's hearts for one extra trick given the likely 4-2 division, you will need two outside dummy entries, which you have: the ♠J and the ♣K. However, you still have to be careful. After you win the ◊A, you can afford to play the ♠A and then the ace and king of hearts and ruff a heart, noticing the 4-2 division. Now the key play: continue with a spade to the jack, using the trump entry *before* the side-suit entry, and ruff another heart. establishing dummy's fifth heart. Now draw the last trump, cross to dummy with the ♣K and discard the losing diamond on the fifth heart. Whew! Had you crossed to the ♣K first and saved the ♠J for later, you would not have made the hand; the opponents would still have had a trump.

Key point

- If you have a 5-2 side suit along with enough dummy entries to set up the suit for just one discard, you have a near 85% chance of success.

Hand 3 *Eenie, meenie, miney, moe*

North
- ♠ J 10 8
- ♡ A K 7
- ◊ K J 8 7 5
- ♣ K Q

West
- ♠ 5 3
- ♡ Q 10 9 8
- ◊ 3 2
- ♣ J 10 9 7 4

East
- ♠ 7 6
- ♡ 6 3 2
- ◊ Q 10 9
- ♣ A 6 5 3 2

South (You)
- ♠ A K Q 9 4 2
- ♡ J 5 4
- ◊ A 6 4
- ♣ 8

	BOTH VUL		DEALER NORTH	
West	**North**	**East**	**South**
	1NT	pass	3♠[1]
pass	4♡[2]	pass	4NT[3]
pass	5◊[4]	pass	6♠
all pass			

1. BLT (Before lovely transfers).
2. Cuebid in support of spades.
3. Regular Blackwood.
4. One ace.

Opening Lead: ♣J

Say that East wins the ♣A and returns a club, affording you a discard. Careful! Discard a diamond, not a heart. Now, after trumps are removed, establish dummy's diamonds (without needing a finesse) for a heart discard. If you discard a heart, you will still lose a diamond; but if you discard a diamond, you will not lose a heart.

Key point
- As declarer, when faced with a choice of discarding a loser from one of two suits, discard the loser from dummy's longer suit. That in turn may allow you to set up dummy's long suit and then discard your other loser(s).

EAST-WEST VUL.		DEALER SOUTH	
West	**North**	**East**	**South**
			2♣
pass	2♢	pass	2♡
pass	3♣[1]	pass	3♡[2]
pass	4♡[3]	all pass	

1. Double negative, denying as much as a king.
2. Not forcing – asking partner for a possible trick.
3. Hoping a diamond ruff in dummy will be that trick.

Opening lead: ♣K

Hand 4 *A dummy only a mother could love*

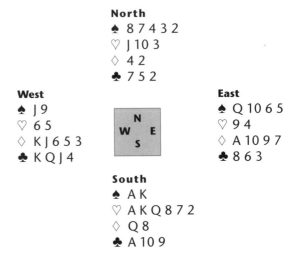

North
♠ 8 7 4 3 2
♡ J 10 3
♢ 4 2
♣ 7 5 2

West
♠ J 9
♡ 6 5
♢ K J 6 5 3
♣ K Q J 4

East
♠ Q 10 6 5
♡ 9 4
♢ A 10 9 7
♣ 8 6 3

South
♠ A K
♡ A K Q 8 7 2
♢ Q 8
♣ A 10 9

With four minor-suit losers, you are going to have to work with dummy's 'powerful' spade suit using hearts as the 'communications' suit. The problem is that spades will probably break 4-2, in which case you are going to need three dummy entries. Can you see three? They are available, if the opponents' hearts break 2-2.

Cash the ♠AK at Tricks 2 and 3 and carefully cross to dummy's ♡10 using the seven or the eight. Don't even think of using the deuce! Ruff a spade with a high honor, cross back to dummy with the ♡J, ruff a second spade high, and return to dummy with the ♡3, using your 'jewel in the crown', the ♡2, to get to dummy a third time. Now, finally, you can disgorge one minor-suit loser on dummy's fifth spade.

Had spades divided 3-3, you would only need to ruff one spade in your hand. After ruffing a spade and noticing the 3-3 division, your plan should be to draw trumps ending in dummy (play a high trump and then a low one to dummy in case hearts are 3-1) so you can use both spades.

Key point
• When you are establishing dummy's length and your only entries to dummy are in the trump suit, it behooves you to save a trump that is lower than dummy's lowest trump as you may need that trump to get over there in the endgame.

Test yourself

Part 1

In this section you are South and dummy is North. Hearts are trumps and your dummy has a side suit of spades. You will be told how that side suit breaks. Your job is to determine how many dummy entries you are going to need in order to set up the suit — keeping in mind that you have to include the final entry which allows you to get over there to use the established winner(s).

1.

North (Dummy)

♠ 8 7 5 4 3 2

N	
W	E
S	

South (You)

♠ A

How many dummy entries do you need to set up this suit if their spades divide (a) 3-3, (b) 4-2, (c) 5-1?

Solution on page 71

2.

North

♠ A 9 7 6 3 2

N	
W	E
S	

South

♠ 5 4

Assuming spades are known to be 3-2, how many dummy entries, excluding the ♠A, do you need to set up this suit?

Solution on page 71

3.

North

♠ 9 7 6 4 3

N	
W	E
S	

South

♠ A K

Assuming spades are 4-2, how many dummy entries do you need to set up this suit?

Solution on page 71

4.

North
♠ 10 9 7 6 4 3 2

South
♠ —

Solution on page 71

Assuming spades are 3-3, how many dummy entries do you need to set up this suit?

5.

North
♠ A 10 6 5

South
♠ 4

Solution on page 71

Can this suit possibly produce two tricks? If so, what adverse holding do you need to find?

6.

North
♠ A 9 8 5 3 2

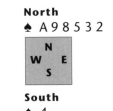

South
♠ 4

a) In order to develop a total of four tricks from this suit, how must the suit be divided?

b) If the East-West spades are divided 4-2, how many tricks can you get from the suit?

c) If the East-West spades are divided 4-2, how many dummy entries (including the ♠A) do you need to set up the suit?

Solutions on page 71

Part 2

The object of this exercise is twofold: (1) To help you count dummy entries; (2) To make you realize that if you don't have enough dummy entries, you shouldn't spin your wheels and embark on a plan that can't possibly work! In the following five problems, plan the play, paying particular attention to entries, and see if your solution jibes with the 'official' solution.

1. Touchy small slam!

North (Dummy)
♠ 8
♡ A J 5 4 2
♢ A J 7 6 4 3
♣ A

```
    N
 W     E
    S
```

South (You)
♠ A K 10 9 7 6 5
♡ 10 9 6
♢ 9
♣ K Q

	BOTH VUL.		DEALER SOUTH
West	**North**	**East**	**South**
			1♠
pass	2♢	pass	2♠
pass	3♡	pass	4♠
pass	6♠	all pass	

West leads the ♣J. You have to count on at least one trump loser. How do you play so as to avoid a heart loser as well?

Solution on page 72

2. Touchy grand slam!

North (Dummy)
♠ Q 8
♡ K 7 6 4 3
♢ K 6 5
♢ 10 6 5

```
    N
 W     E
    S
```

South (You)
♠ A K J 9 6 5 4
♡ A
♢ A 7 4
♣ A 7

	NEITHER VUL.		DEALER SOUTH
West	**North**	**East**	**South**
			2♣[1]
pass	2♡	pass	2♠
pass	3♠	pass	4NT[2]
pass	5♣	pass	5NT
pass	6♡	pass	7♠[3]
all pass			

1.	Strong and artificial.
2.	Regular Blackwood.
3.	Where there are 12, there must be 13.

West leads the ♢Q. What is your plan?

Solution on page 73

3. Jewel in the crown

EAST-WEST VUL.		DEALER SOUTH	
West	**North**	**East**	**South**
			2♣
pass	2◇[1]	pass	3♣
pass	3♠	pass	4♣[2]
pass	4♠[3]	pass	6♣
all pass			

1. Waiting.
2. Agreeing clubs as the trump suit.
3. Cuebid.

Opening lead: ◇Q

Solutions on page 74

North (Dummy)
♠ A 8 5 4 2
♡ 8 7 6
◇ 7 4
♣ 10 8 3

South (You)
♠ 3
♡ A Q 9
◇ A K
♣ A K Q J 9 4 2

a) How do you play if their clubs are divided 2-1?
b) How do you play if West has all three missing trumps?

4. Technique is the answer

NEITHER VUL.		DEALER SOUTH	
West	**North**	**East**	**South**
			2♡[1]
pass	2NT[2]	pass	3◇[3]
pass	4♡	all pass	

1. Weak.
2. Asking for more information.
3. Feature.

Opening lead: ◇J

Solution on page 75

North (Dummy)
♠ J 9 6 5 3
♡ K Q
◇ K 4 2
♣ A J 6

South (You)
♠ 2
♡ A J 10 8 6 4
◇ A 7 5
♣ 10 3 2

When the opponents first gain the lead, a diamond will be returned. Plan the play.

5. What's the catch? (double credit for this one!)

North (Dummy)
♠ Q 9 2
♡ A K 8 6 4 3
♢ 6 2
♣ A K

	N	
W		E
	S	

South (You)
♠ A K J 10 7 4
♡ 9 2
♢ A Q 5 4
♣ 7

Plan the play.

BOTH VUL.		DEALER SOUTH	
West	**North**	**East**	**South**
			1♠
pass	2♡	pass	3♠
pass	4♣[1]	pass	4♢[2]
pass	4NT	pass	5♢[3]
pass	7♠	all pass	

1. Presumed cuebids for spades.
2. Roman Keycard Blackwood.
3. 3 Keycards.

Opening lead: ♣J

Solution on page 76

Test yourself — solutions

Part 1

1. a) If spades break 3-3, you need three dummy entries; two to get to dummy to trump spades, one to get back to use the established spades.

b) If spades break 4-2, you need four dummy entries; three to get to dummy to trump spades, one to get back to use the established spades.

c) If spades break 5-1, you need five dummy entries; four to get to dummy to ruff spades, one to get back to use the established spade. Good luck!

2. One! Duck a spade (the key play), and later play the ace of spades and ruff a spade. Now you only need one side dummy entry to get back and use the spades. If you play the ace of spades and another spade, you will need two side dummy entries to establish the suit.

3. Three. Two to enter dummy to trump spades; one more to get back to use the established spade.

4. Four. Three to enter dummy to ruff spades; one more to get back to use the established spades.

5. Yes, if either hand has specifically ♠KQJ alone.

6. a) 3-3 b) Three c) Four. After you play the ♠A (one entry) and ruff a spade, you have to get back to dummy two more times to trump spades (two more entries) and then you have to get over there a fourth time to use the established spades.

BOTH VUL.   DEALER SOUTH

West	North	East	South
			1♠
pass	2◇	pass	2♠
pass	3♡	pass	4♠
pass	6♠	all pass	

West leads the ♣J

Part 2

1.

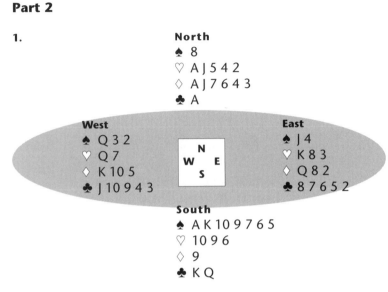

North
♠ 8
♡ A J 5 4 2
◇ A J 7 6 4 3
♣ A

West
♠ Q 3 2
♡ Q 7
◇ K 10 5
♣ J 10 9 4 3

East
♠ J 4
♡ K 8 3
◇ Q 8 2
♣ 8 7 6 5 2

South
♠ A K 10 9 7 6 5
♡ 10 9 6
◇ 9
♣ K Q

This is sort of a sneaky one. What you have to do is set up the diamonds for heart pitches — not easy. Win the opening lead in dummy (nice play), play the ace of diamonds and ruff a diamond. Next, *ruff your winning club* in order to ruff a second diamond. If diamonds break 3-3, you have three good diamonds over there. In order to make sure you can use them, play the ace and king and a third spade, hoping to remove all of the opponents' spades. As it happens, spades are 3-2 and diamonds are 3-3 (am I good to you, or what?) and you make your slam.

Key points
- Sometimes you have to trump your own good tricks to get to dummy.
- When a side suit is established by ruffing, you can't use it until you remove all of their trumps.

2.

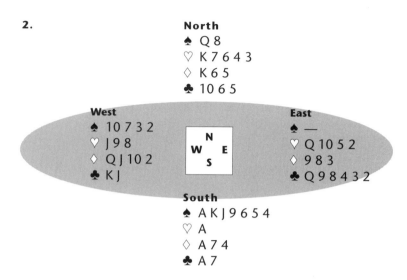

North
♠ Q 8
♡ K 7 6 4 3
♢ K 6 5
♣ 10 6 5

West
♠ 10 7 3 2
♡ J 9 8
♢ Q J 10 2
♣ K J

East
♠ —
♡ Q 10 5 2
♢ 9 8 3
♣ Q 9 8 4 3 2

South
♠ A K J 9 6 5 4
♡ A
♢ A 7 4
♣ A 7

NEITHER VUL.		DEALER SOUTH	
West	**North**	**East**	**South**
			2♣[1]
pass	2♡	pass	2♠
pass	3♠	pass	4NT[2]
pass	5♣	pass	5NT
pass	6♡	pass	7♠[3]
all pass			

1. Strong and artificial.
2. Regular Blackwood.
3. Where there are 12, there must be 13.

West leads the ♢Q

You have twelve top tricks and have to come up with a thirteenth. The only place you can get it is by setting up a fifth heart in dummy, which will require their hearts to break 4-3 (a 63 % shot, by the way). In order to set up that fifth heart, you need three, count 'em, three dummy entries: two to get over to trump hearts and one more to get back there to use the winning heart.

Ostensibly dummy has only two entries, but if West has the ♠10, you can lead a spade to the eight and develop a third entry. Since it is about your only chance, you might as well go for it. Win the opening lead in your hand, conserving the ♢K for later, much later, and cash the ♡A. Now for your big play, a spade to the eight. It wins! Ruff a low heart, return to the ♠Q, ruff another low heart, draw the three remaining trumps with your ♠AKJ, and finally, cross to the ♢K and deposit your losing diamond and your losing club on the ♡K7.

Key points
- At times you may have to take a finesse in a suit in which you have no losers in order to build up an extra dummy entry; it only hurts for a little while.
- When establishing dummy's long suit, such as the heart suit in this hand, it is safer to ruff low hearts twice without cashing the king first because you absolutely need a 4-3 heart break. However, if you wanted to verify early that hearts were breaking 4-3, and your trump suit was strong enough to ruff two hearts in any case, cash the ♡K and then ruff a heart. Now, if hearts turn out to be 5-2, maybe you can try something else.

EAST-WEST VUL.		DEALER SOUTH	
West	**North**	**East**	**South**
			2♣
pass	2◇[1]	pass	3♣
pass	3♠	pass	4♣[2]
pass	4♠[3]	pass	6♣
all pass			

1.   Waiting.
2.   Agreeing clubs as the trump suit.
3.   Cuebid.

West leads the ◇Q

3.

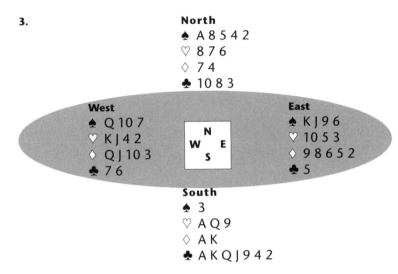

```
                North
                ♠ A 8 5 4 2
                ♡ 8 7 6
                ◇ 7 4
                ♣ 10 8 3
West                              East
♠ Q 10 7            N             ♠ K J 9 6
♡ K J 4 2       W       E         ♡ 10 5 3
◇ Q J 10 3          S             ◇ 9 8 6 5 2
♣ 7 6                             ♣ 5
                South
                ♠ 3
                ♡ A Q 9
                ◇ A K
                ♣ A K Q J 9 4 2
```

With eleven top tricks (always count your tricks), you need to develop one more. There is always the possibility of developing a long spade in dummy if the suit divides 4-3, if you have enough dummy entries. Do you?

If, when you trump the third spade from dummy, you see the spades are breaking 5-2, use your two remaining dummy entries to finesse in hearts. The proper way to play hearts for two tricks is to lead low to the nine and then, if that loses to the ten or jack, lead low to the queen. If their trumps are divided 3-0, which means you don't have enough dummy entries to set up the spades even if they break 4-3, switch your attention to hearts. Again, first finesse the nine and then the queen.

You will need three dummy entries to set up those spades. If their clubs are divided 2-1, you have them — your ♣2 (the jewel in your crown) can be used to get to the ♣3 eventually! It should go like this: Win the opening lead, play the ace of spades and ruff a spade high, very high. Return to dummy with the ♣8 and if both opponents follow, ruff another spade high. If spades are 4-3, return to dummy with the ♣10 (saving the 'jewel' for later), ruff another spade (but not with the 'jewel') and finally use the 'jewel' to get to dummy to use the long spade to discard the ♡9. Now you can take the heart finesse, trying for an overtrick. No luck.

Key points

- With a powerful trump suit and a limited number of dummy entries in the trump suit, be sure to save a lower trump to enable you to get to dummy as many times as possible.
- The best play for two tricks with the AQ9 facing xx or xxx is to lead low to the nine and then low to the queen.

4.

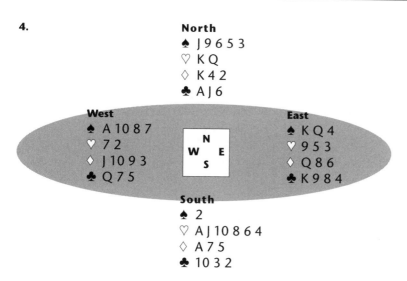

North
♠ J 9 6 5 3
♡ K Q
◇ K 4 2
♣ A J 6

West
♠ A 10 8 7
♥ 7 2
◇ J 10 9 3
♣ Q 7 5

East
♠ K Q 4
♥ 9 5 3
◇ Q 8 6
♣ K 9 8 4

South
♠ 2
♡ A J 10 8 6 4
◇ A 7 5
♣ 10 3 2

NEITHER VUL.   DEALER SOUTH

West	North	East	South
			2♡[1]
pass	2NT[2]	pass	3◇[3]
pass	4♡	all pass	

1. Weak.
2. Asking for more information.
3. Feature.

The opening lead is the ◇J.

Here we go again. Four likely losers: one spade, one diamond, and two clubs, plus another pathetic five-card spade suit in dummy. However, to counterbalance the weak spades there are four dummy entries and a strong trump suit to back up the procedure. Start on the spades!

Win the ◇A and lead a spade. Win the diamond return, and trump a spade low. Now it is important to cross to dummy twice in hearts and ruff two more spades. Then remove the outstanding trump, cross to the ace of clubs (or finesse the jack — they can only take one diamond and you will be able to discard your other club on the fifth spade), and discard a minor-suit loser on the fifth spade.

Key points
- After you have decided to set up dummy's long suit, start with the suit immediately — no, sooner.
- When there are multiple dummy entries and you are setting up a side suit, use the trump entries first and save the side-suit entry for last. This is a recording.
- Keep track of the suit you are establishing so you know when it is good, or know when the suit breaks so obscenely that it cannot be set up.

BOTH VUL.   DEALER SOUTH

West	North	East	South
			1♠
pass	2♡	pass	3♠
pass	4♣[1]	pass	4♢[2]
pass	4NT	pass	5♢[3]
pass	7♠	all pass	

1. Presumed cuebids for spades.
2. Roman Keycard Blackwood with 1430 responses.
3. 3 Key Cards.

Opening lead: ♣J

5.

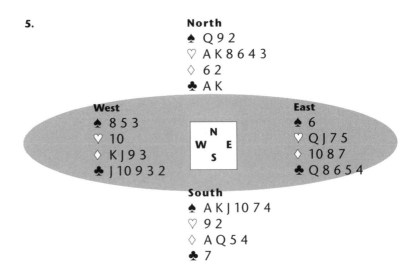

North
♠ Q 9 2
♡ A K 8 6 4 3
♢ 6 2
♣ A K

West
♠ 8 5 3
♡ 10
♢ K J 9 3
♣ J 10 9 3 2

East
♠ 6
♡ Q J 7 5
♢ 10 8 7
♣ Q 8 6 5 4

South
♠ A K J 10 7 4
♡ 9 2
♢ A Q 5 4
♣ 7

Clearly you must work with dummy's hearts to pitch your diamonds. Don't even think of taking the diamond finesse with that heart suit over there along with two spade entries. The catch is that hearts might divide 4-1 and you might get a heart honor trumped. After all you can't draw trumps first, because the trumps are going to serve as eventual entries to the hearts.

You do, however, have a neat safety play at your disposal. Play a second club and discard a heart. Now play the ♡A and trump a heart high. If both opponents have followed suit, all of dummy's hearts are high and you can draw trumps ending in dummy and run the hearts. If hearts have divided 4-1 as in the diagram, enter dummy again with the ♠9, ruff another heart high, and then play the ace of spades and another spade to dummy's queen. Dummy is left with three winning hearts, just what the doctor ordered to get rid of your three losing diamonds.

Key points

- Every so often you can take out a little insurance when you have the ace-king of a long suit facing a small doubleton in your hand. If you can discard one of your two small cards before starting your long suit establishment, you may be able to overcome a bad break in the suit.
- When you have eight cards in your long suit between your hand and dummy, you can expect a 3-2 break 68% of the time. However, you can also expect a 4-1 break 28% of the time.

Key ideas from Chapter 2

- One of the two main ways of ridding yourself of losers at suit contracts is to **establish winners** in a long suit by ruffing.
- When establishing a long suit in dummy, the key word is **entries**. You must have enough dummy entries to get over there to ruff the suit you are establishing plus one more to get over to use it.
- When establishing a long suit by ruffing, you must be able to draw trumps before using the winners you have set up.
- If the only entries to dummy are in the trump suit, use the **trump entries** to set up the long suit; do not draw trumps prematurely.
- When trumping dummy's long suit, if you have a plethora of high trumps, do not be miserly — ruff high so that you can't be overruffed.
- If extra entries to dummy are needed to set up a long suit, you may have to take a seemingly risky finesse (perhaps even with a solid trump suit) to get over there one extra time. Do it!
- If the only entries to dummy are in the trump suit, and there are not enough trumps in dummy to be able to draw trumps ending in dummy, forget the whole thing. It's not going to work.
- If dummy has both trump entries and side-suit entries, use the trump entries first.
- As there is some risk involved in setting up a side suit, be careful about using this technique if it is simply a matter of overtricks. However, playing matchpoints, where overtricks are important, take the risk.
- If dummy does not have sufficient entries to set up the long suit, or if the bidding tells you that the suit is breaking too foully to be established, look for an alternative line of play.
- When holding a small doubleton facing Axxxx(x) in the suit you are planning to develop, duck the first round of the suit; it saves an entry.
- When holding a combined total of seven cards between your hand and dummy, expect a 4-2 break 48% of the time and a 3-3 break 36% of the time. When holding eight cards between your hand and dummy, expect a 3-2 break 68% of the time and a 4-1 break 28% of the time.

When Not To Finesse

Two roads diverged in the wood, and I —
I took the one less traveled by...

ROBERT FROST

Show me a player who goes out of the way to avoid a finesse and I will show you a winning player. Most players love to take finesses. Some are so enamored with the whole process that they even take finesses that are not necessary. These finesses are called 'practice finesses'. A practice finesse is a finesse which if it works doesn't gain you a trick, but if it loses, it costs you either a trick or your contract! As we all know, a finesse is not a sure thing, so if you can find a way to avoid or even postpone one until alternative channels are explored, you're on the right track. The following examples illustrate some of these 'alternative channels'. They will be presented to you as problems, so when you see the

sign, stop and think before reading on. If no bidding is given, that's because it is irrelevant. In other words, you are on your own!

Finesse avoidance techniques

When two finesses are available

NEITHER VUL.		DEALER SOUTH	
West	**North**	**East**	**South**
			1♡
pass	2NT[1]	pass	3NT
pass	4♡	all pass	

1. 13-15 balanced, could contain 4-card trump support (not Jacoby).

North (Dummy)
♠ 9 8 7
♡ A J 10 3
◇ Q J 10
♣ A Q 10

South (You)
♠ A Q
♡ K Q 9 8 7
◇ 7 5 4 3
♣ J 3

You are declarer in 4♡. The opening lead is the ◇2; East wins the ace and returns a diamond to West's king; West plays a third diamond, East ruffs and exits with a low spade. Should you finesse?

Only if practice finesses are your bag. Even if the spade finesse works, you still need the club finesse. But if the club finesse works, it can be repeated and a spade can be discarded on a winning club. In other words, you don't need the spade finesse — it's a trap!

If a winning finesse in a relatively long, strong suit means not needing a finesse in a weaker suit, take the finesse in the stronger suit. Why take two finesses when one will do quite nicely, thank you?

Here's the full deal:

North (Dummy)
♠ 9 8 7
♡ A J 10 3
♢ Q J 10
♣ A Q 10

West
♠ K 6 5 3
♡ 4 2
♢ K 9 6 2
♣ K 9 8

East
♠ J 10 4 2
♡ 6 5
♢ A 8
♣ 7 6 5 4 2

South (You)
♠ A Q
♡ K Q 9 8 7
♢ 7 5 4 3
♣ J 3

Giving yourself that extra chance

North (Dummy)
♠ J 9 8
♡ A K 10 3
♢ Q J 10
♣ A Q 4

South (You)
♠ A K
♡ Q J 9 8 7
♢ 5 4 3 2
♣ 7 3

Again you are declarer in 4♡, and again the lead is a diamond, this time the ace. When this holds the first trick, West continues with the king and then plays a third diamond which East ruffs (these guys are tough). East exits with a spade. See any way of avoiding the club finesse?

On this hand you'll probably have to finesse in clubs eventually, but it can't cost to draw trumps and play a second high spade first, just in case the ♠ Q drops. If it does, your club loser goes on the ♠ J; if it doesn't, take the club finesse.

Before taking a finesse, make sure there is no possibility of setting up a side suit discard that makes the finesse unnecessary. If the discard possibility doesn't work out, take the finesse.

The whole deal:

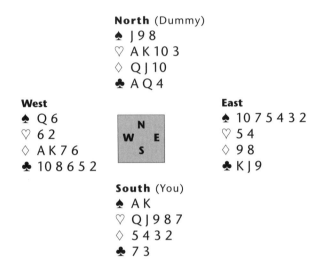

North (Dummy)
♠ J 9 8
♡ A K 10 3
◇ Q J 10
♣ A Q 4

West
♠ Q 6
♡ 6 2
◇ A K 7 6
♣ 10 8 6 5 2

East
♠ 10 7 5 4 3 2
♡ 5 4
◇ 9 8
♣ K J 9

South (You)
♠ A K
♡ Q J 9 8 7
◇ 5 4 3 2
♣ 7 3

Now see if you can spot the extra chances that are available on this next hand:

North
♠ A K J 2
♡ K 6 3
◇ 7 5 2
♣ K Q 7

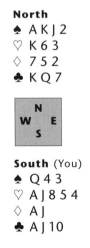

South (You)
♠ Q 4 3
♡ A J 8 5 4
◇ A J
♣ A J 10

You alight in 6♡ and West leads a nasty ◇K. Any ideas?

Rather than put all your eggs in one basket and take the heart finesse, give yourself two chances. First, win the ◊A and play off the king and ace of hearts. Assuming no queen drops, you plan to cash spades and throw your diamond away – you will still survive if the player with the ♡Q has at least three spades. Of course, a little bit of chicanery can't hurt. Cross to the ♠ A, cash the ♠ K, and (oh, so cleverly) lead a low spade toward your queen. If East has the ♡Q and a doubleton spade, East may be duped into thinking you are about to trump and may discard instead ruffing. Now you can win the ♠ Q, cross to dummy with a club, and discard your losing diamond on the ♠ J. Applause.

When you have to get rid of a loser without letting the opponents in, and you have a trump suit missing the queen plus a side suit that may furnish a discard for your loser, consider playing the ace-king of trumps. If the queen doesn't drop, then try getting rid of your loser on the side suit. Of course this means that you need the player with the high trump not to be short in the side suit.

The full deal:

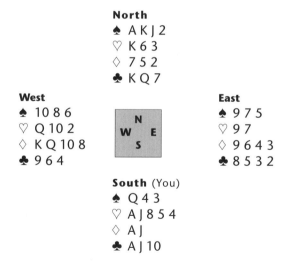

North
♠ A K J 2
♡ K 6 3
◊ 7 5 2
♣ K Q 7

West
♠ 10 8 6
♡ Q 10 2
◊ K Q 10 8
♣ 9 6 4

East
♠ 9 7 5
♡ 9 7
◊ 9 6 4 3
♣ 8 5 3 2

South (You)
♠ Q 4 3
♡ A J 8 5 4
◊ A J
♣ A J 10

Establishable side suits

This should be easy after you have toiled through the previous chapter!

BOTH VUL.		DEALER NORTH	
West	**North**	**East**	**South**
	pass	pass	1♡
pass	2♡	pass	4♡
all pass			

North (Dummy)
♠ 10 8
♡ Q J 10
♢ 6 4 3
♣ K 9 7 6 4

South (You)
♠ A Q
♡ A K 9 8 6 2
♢ J 9 8
♣ A 3

Yes, again you are playing 4♡, and yes, again the opening lead is the ♢K (how little imagination these bridge authors have!). West continues with the diamond queen and then a third diamond to East's ace. East shifts to a spade. Should you finesse?

If there were no place to get rid of the ♠Q, of course you would finesse. But you have a great chance to establish at least one of dummy's clubs for a spade discard. If clubs break 3-3 (36%) or 4-2 (48%), you can establish a club for a spade pitch. An 84% is better than a 50% chance.

Win the ♠A, play the ♣AK and ruff a club high. If clubs break 3-3, draw trumps ending in dummy and pitch the ♠Q on a club. If clubs turn out to be 4-2, enter dummy with a trump, ruff another club high, draw trumps ending in dummy, and once again discard that temptress, the ♠Q, on dummy's fifth club.

If the odds, entries, and time are on your side, go for long suit establishment rather than finessing. In an ideal world, you have time to try and develop your long suit, and failing that, take a finesse. However, if you have to make an early decision, fall back on simple percentages.

The chance of establishing a side suit divided 5-2, no matter how weak, for one discard are almost 85%, which makes it a much better shot than a finesse. All you need is vision and entries! However, if the choice is between playing for a 3-3 division (36%) or taking a finesse, and you have to make an early decision, go for the finesse.

The full deal:

North (Dummy)
♠ 10 8
♡ Q J 10
♢ 6 4 3
♣ K 9 7 6 4

West
♠ K 7 5
♡ 7 5 3
♢ K Q 10
♣ Q 10 8 5

East
♠ J 9 6 4 3 2
♡ 4
♢ A 7 5 2
♣ J 2

South (You)
♠ A Q
♡ A K 9 8 6 2
♢ J 9 8
♣ A 3

Taking a second look at equal-length side suits with finesse possibilities

North (Dummy)
♠ A Q
♡ K Q 7 6 5
♢ Q 7 2
♣ 9 8 7

South (You)
♠ 3 2
♡ A J 10 9 8
♢ J 6 5
♣ A K Q

BOTH VUL.		DEALER SOUTH	
West	**North**	**East**	**South**
			1♡
pass	2NT[1]	pass	3♡[2]
pass	3♠	pass	4♣
pass	4♡	all pass	

1. Game raise in hearts.
2. No shortness.

Surprise — you are declarer in 4♡. However, this time the opening lead is the ♠ 4. Should you finesse?

Only a masochist or a finessaholic even dreams of finessing here. Spades is an equal-length side suit, and can be used as your throw-in suit (we're going to talk about this at much greater length in Chapter 6). In many end-positions, you can **throw in** a defender by losing a trick to him at the right time; if everything has worked out, he may have to lead a suit that will help you.

Win the ♠A, draw trumps, play three rounds of clubs, and exit with the ♠Q. The opponent with the ♠K will be forced to break diamonds, giving you a diamond trick or to concede an equally ruinous ruff and sluff. Either way, you wind up losing two diamonds and a spade. Meanwhile back at the ranch, if you finesse the spade and it loses, you are very likely to lose three diamonds and a spade. Why take practice finesses when you have a sure thing?

Assuming a hand can be stripped, and you have a side suit you would rather the opponents broach, consider using your equal-length side suit as your throw-in suit even if it means foregoing a beloved finesse in that suit.

> When you have an equal-length suit with finesse possibilities, pretend the finessable card (♠Q) is a small card and ask yourself how you would play the hand if it were.

The full deal:

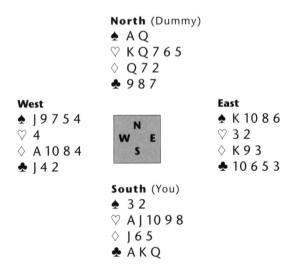

North (Dummy)
♠ A Q
♡ K Q 7 6 5
♢ Q 7 2
♣ 9 8 7

West
♠ J 9 7 5 4
♡ 4
♢ A 10 8 4
♣ J 4 2

East
♠ K 10 8 6
♡ 3 2
♢ K 9 3
♣ 10 6 5 3

South (You)
♠ 3 2
♡ A J 10 9 8
♢ J 6 5
♣ A K Q

Using your trump suit as your throw-in suit

North
♠ K Q 4
♡ 8 5
♢ J 10 5 4
♣ A 8 7 4

South (You)
♠ A 7 6
♡ 4
♢ A Q 9 8 7 2
♣ K J 10

EAST-WEST VUL.		DEALER SOUTH	
West	**North**	**East**	**South**
			1♢
pass	3♢	pass	5♢
all pass			

You arrive at 5♢, West leads the ♡K, East signals encouragement, and West continues with the ♡Q which you ruff. Now what?

You have a possible trump loser, a possible club loser, and finesse possibilities in both suits. The percentage play in diamonds is to finesse, but that is just considering the diamond suit in isolation (as if there was no other problem). But there is another problem — the club suit. Who are you going to play for the club queen?

There is (remember the title of this chapter?) a better way. In order to avoid the unpleasantness of guessing (or worse, misguessing) the ♣Q, why not let your opponents do your dirty work? Lay down the ♢A and, assuming both opponents follow but no king appears, cash your three high spades. If nobody ruffs, exit with a trump. Whoever has the king, must break clubs for you or concede a ruff and sluff. (If someone ruffs a spade, that someone will find himself in the same position.)

Even though it has finesse possibilities, if your trump suit can be used as a throw-in suit to avoid a guess in another suit, abandon the trump finesse. It only hurts for a little while.

The full deal:

North (Dummy)
♠ K Q 4
♡ 8 5
◇ J 10 5 4
♣ A 8 7 4

West
♠ J 9 5 3
♡ K Q J 9
◇ K 6
♣ 9 3 2

East
♠ 10 8 2
♡ A 10 7 6 3 2
◇ 3
♣ Q 6 5

South (You)
♠ A 7 6
♡ 4
◇ A Q 9 8 7 2
♣ K J 10

Looking for a winner in an unusual place

NEITHER VUL.		DEALER EAST	
West	**North**	**East**	**South**
		pass	1♣
pass	1♠	pass	2♡
pass	3♣[1]	pass	4♣[2]
pass	4♠[3]	pass	6♣
all pass			

1. Game Force.
2. RKB after a 3-level game forcing agreement.
3. Two keycards without the trump queen.

North (Dummy)
♠ A Q 10 9 8
♡ 3
◇ J 8 6 4
♣ K 9 8

South (You)
♠ J 2
♡ A K Q J
◇ K
♣ A Q J 10 3 2

For a change of pace, the contract is 6♣; however, the opening lead is the ◇2. East wins the ◇A and switches to a heart. Can you see any way to avoid the spade finesse?

Before attempting the spade finesse, enter dummy twice in clubs and trump diamonds. Maybe the queen will fall... if it doesn't, take the spade finesse.

Trying to ruff out a missing honor before taking a finesse is another way of giving yourself an extra chance.

The full deal:

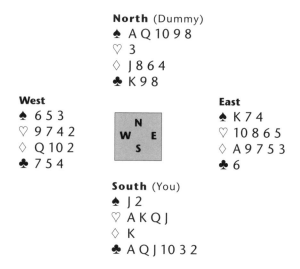

North (Dummy)
♠ A Q 10 9 8
♡ 3
◇ J 8 6 4
♣ K 9 8

West
♠ 6 5 3
♡ 9 7 4 2
◇ Q 10 2
♣ 7 5 4

East
♠ K 7 4
♡ 10 8 6 5
◇ A 9 7 5 3
♣ 6

South (You)
♠ J 2
♡ A K Q J
◇ K
♣ A Q J 10 3 2

Two chances are better than one

North (Dummy)
♠ A K 9 8
♡ 2
◇ A Q J 4 3
♣ K 8 6

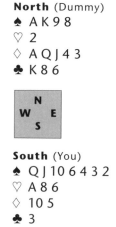

South (You)
♠ Q J 10 6 4 3 2
♡ A 8 6
◇ 10 5
♣ 3

| | NEITHER VUL. | DEALER SOUTH | |
West	**North**	**East**	**South**
			3♠
pass	4NT[1]	pass	5♣[2]
pass	6♠	all pass	

1. RKB .
2. One keycard.

Happy to find you with an ace, partner tries for slam. West leads the ♡Q. See any way to avoid the diamond finesse?

After drawing trumps, try leading a club toward the king before playing on diamonds. If West has the ♣ A, you won't need the diamond finesse. Your losing diamond goes away on the ♣K. If East has the ♣A, you can still fall back on the diamond finesse. If you take the diamond finesse first and it loses, you will lose a club and a diamond. One finesse is a 50-50 proposition; one of two finesses is a 75% chance.

Assuming you can afford to lose one trick and need only one discard, leading a singleton toward a king can be a neat way of avoiding a finesse in another suit. If the king loses to the ace, you can always take the other finesse. If the ace is well-placed, you won't need the other finesse.

The full deal:

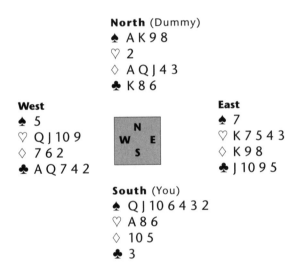

North (Dummy)
♠ A K 9 8
♡ 2
◇ A Q J 4 3
♣ K 8 6

West
♠ 5
♡ Q J 10 9
◇ 7 6 2
♣ A Q 7 4 2

East
♠ 7
♡ K 7 5 4 3
◇ K 9 8
♣ J 10 9 5

South (You)
♠ Q J 10 6 4 3 2
♡ A 8 6
◇ 10 5
♣ 3

When dummy has a void

North (Dummy)
♠ —
♡ A Q 10 9 7 4
◊ 7 3 2
♣ A K 5 4

South (You)
♠ K 8
♡ K J 8 3 2
◊ A Q 5 4
♣ 7 6

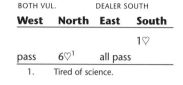

		BOTH VUL.	DEALER SOUTH	
West	**North**	**East**	**South**	
			1♡	
pass	6♡[1]	all pass		

1. Tired of science.

You are declarer in 6♡ (your opening bid must have turned partner on!). West leads the ♠ Q.

See any way of avoiding the diamond finesse?

There is. Discard a diamond from dummy at Trick 1, and then later discard another diamond on the ♠K after East wins the ♠A. One loser is better than two! You wind up losing one spade, but no diamonds. If you ruff the opening lead in dummy, you still have a sure diamond loser, and will need to find East with the ◊K to make your slam.

There is no rule that says you have to ruff an opponent's lead when dummy is void. There are many holdings in your hand, besides the obvious AQ(x) and AKJ, such as Kx(x), KQ(x), or even QJx(x), where discarding from dummy can gain you a trick!

The full deal:

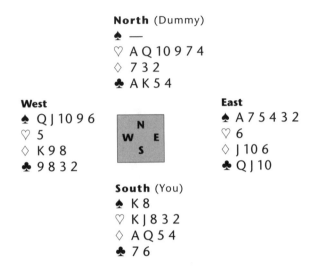

North (Dummy)
♠ —
♡ A Q 10 9 7 4
♢ 7 3 2
♣ A K 5 4

West
♠ Q J 10 9 6
♡ 5
♢ K 9 8
♣ 9 8 3 2

East
♠ A 7 5 4 3 2
♡ 6
♢ J 10 6
♣ Q J 10

South (You)
♠ K 8
♡ K J 8 3 2
♢ A Q 5 4
♣ 7 6

Count your tricks!

NEITHER VUL.		DEALER NORTH	
West	**North**	**East**	**South**
	1♢	pass	1♡
pass	2♡	pass	4♡
all pass			

North (Dummy)
♠ A Q
♡ 10 7 6 3
♢ A K 8 2
♣ 8 7 6

South (You)
♠ 8 6
♡ A K Q 9 2
♢ Q J 3
♣ K 4 2

Back in your familiar contract of 4♡, you see the ♠3 hit the table from West. Should you finesse?

Are you kidding me? As long as West doesn't have ♡Jxxx, you have ten top tricks. Why take a finesse that risks your contract for no reason? What if the finesse loses and a high club comes back through your king? You could lose three clubs and a spade!

Count your winners, even at a suit contract, before you play from dummy at Trick 1. If you have enough top tricks to make your contract, and could be risking your contract by taking an early finesse, don't succumb to temptation. Forget the finesse; take the money and run.

The full deal:

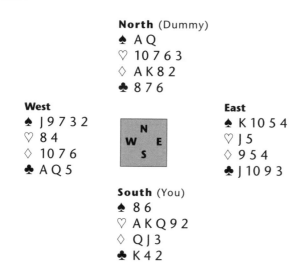

North (Dummy)
♠ A Q
♡ 10 7 6 3
◇ A K 8 2
♣ 8 7 6

West
♠ J 9 7 3 2
♡ 8 4
◇ 10 7 6
♣ A Q 5

East
♠ K 10 5 4
♡ J 5
◇ 9 5 4
♣ J 10 9 3

South (You)
♠ 8 6
♡ A K Q 9 2
◇ Q J 3
♣ K 4 2

Tricks and chances — a necessary combination

NEITHER VUL.		DEALER SOUTH	
West	**North**	**East**	**South**
			2♣
pass	2◊	pass	2NT
pass	6NT	all pass	

North (Dummy)
- ♠ Q 8 4
- ♡ K 8 7 6
- ◊ A Q 9 2
- ♣ 3 2

South (You)
- ♠ A K 5
- ♡ A 5 4
- ◊ K J 4 3
- ♣ A K J

Yes, 6◊ would have been easier, but with two flattish hands and thirty-four high card points between the two hands, you wind up in 6NT. What is your plan? (Remember, this chapter is devoted to avoiding finesses, if possible.)

When trying to establish an extra winner holding Axx facing Kxxx, duck one round, and then play the AK. This technique allows you to retain control of the suit in case of an uneven division.

You have eleven top tricks with two chances of developing a twelfth. If hearts break 3-3, dummy's long heart will be your twelfth trick. If hearts are not 3-3, you can always fall back on the club finesse, so play on hearts before clubs. Cash four diamonds and duck a heart, or duck a heart immediately. Win any return, play the ace and king of hearts, and if they break 3-3, claim. If hearts are not 3-3, take the club finesse. Two chances are better than one.

Before taking a finesse in equal-length suits divided 2-2 or 3-3 (a death-wish finesse) look to develop extra tricks in unevenly divided suits first. If that doesn't work, then fall back on the finesse. Two chances are better than one.

The difference between this and the 4♡ hand on p.84 is that here you can try for long suit establishment and then fall back on a finesse. On that earlier hand, you had to decide whether to take a finesse or go for long suit establishment. Obviously, it is better not to be faced with an early choice. Much better to have time to test the long suit and then take a finesse if the long suit doesn't come in.

The full deal:

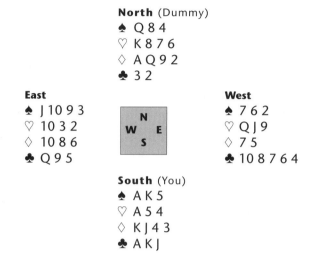

North (Dummy)
♠ Q 8 4
♡ K 8 7 6
♢ A Q 9 2
♣ 3 2

East
♠ J 10 9 3
♡ 10 3 2
♢ 10 8 6
♣ Q 9 5

West
♠ 7 6 2
♡ Q J 9
♢ 7 5
♣ 10 8 7 6 4

South (You)
♠ A K 5
♡ A 5 4
♢ K J 4 3
♣ A K J

I have been using this hand in my Notrump Play class for years. One lady (a faithful return student) went down seven years in a row, always taking the club finesse before ducking a heart and then testing hearts. The eighth year I couldn't stand it any longer; I put the club queen onside and had the hearts break 4-2. So guess what? She played the ace, king and a third heart before touching clubs! Down again!

Resisting temptation

North (Dummy)
♠ K
♡ 7 6 5 4 3 2
♢ 9 6 5
♣ Q J 10

South (You)
♠ A Q J 10 9 2
♡ A Q
♢ A 4 3
♣ A 2

BOTH VUL.		DEALER SOUTH	
West	**North**	**East**	**South**
			2♣
pass	2♢	pass	2♠
pass	3♡	pass	3♠
pass	4♠	all pass	

You are playing in 4♠ and West leads the ♢Q. You start with nine tricks: six spades and three aces. You need one more trick, and you have finesse possibilities in two suits, but only one dummy entry. Eenie meenie miney moe…What's the verdict?

Don't take *either* finesse! If you cross to dummy with a spade and take the heart finesse and it loses, you are stuck with a club loser. If you cross to dummy and take the club finesse and that loses, the clubs are blocked, and you are now stuck with a heart loser.

The simple solution is to win the ♢A, then play ace and a club, setting up one of dummy's clubs for your tenth trick. After the opponents win the ♣K, and have cashed their diamonds, you can cross to dummy with a spade and pitch your ♡Q on a winning club.

When dummy is short of entries, consider abandoning a finesse for the safer option of setting up a winner(s) in dummy, preserving the entry until the winner(s) have been established.

The full deal:

North (Dummy)
♠ K
♡ 7 6 5 4 3 2
♢ 9 6 5
♣ Q J 10

West
♠ 6 4
♡ K 10 8
♢ Q J 10 2
♣ K 9 7 5

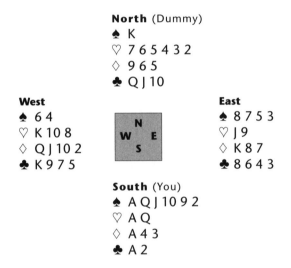

East
♠ 8 7 5 3
♡ J 9
♢ K 8 7
♣ 8 6 4 3

South (You)
♠ A Q J 10 9 2
♡ A Q
♢ A 4 3
♣ A 2

Have you got time?

As we all know, many bridge hands reduce themselves down to a race. The defense is trying to set up a trick (maybe the setting trick), while you are trying desperately to get rid of that loser before they prevail. This mad race may mean putting a finesse on hold or even abandoning a tempting one altogether!

North
♠ J 10 9 3
♡ A 8 5
◇ 10 7 5 4
♣ Q 7

South (You)
♠ A Q 8 7 4
♡ K 6 3
◇ K
♣ A 8 4 2

		NEITHER VUL.	DEALER SOUTH
West	**North**	**East**	**South**
			1♠
dbl	3♠	pass	4♠
all pass			

Opening lead: ♡Q

Faced with a possible loser in each suit, and two suits that can be finessed, what is your plan?

The first order of business is to try to get rid of that heart loser. Win the opening lead in your hand and lead a low club. If, as expected from the auction, West has the king and takes it, you will have established a potential heart discard from dummy on the ♣A.

Assume West wins his club king and exits with a heart to dummy's ace. Cash the ♣Q, then show some maturity and cross to the ♠A (no finessing, please) to get to your hand quickly in order to discard dummy's remaining heart on the ♣A. Now you can ruff a heart in dummy and lead a diamond. As long as the player with the ◇A doesn't have both remaining spades (unlikely), you will be able to ruff your club loser in dummy.

The full deal:

North
♠ J 10 9 3
♡ A 8 5
◇ 10 7 5 4
♣ Q 7

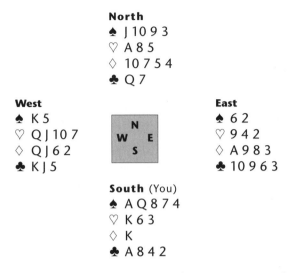

West
♠ K 5
♡ Q J 10 7
◇ Q J 6 2
♣ K J 5

East
♠ 6 2
♡ 9 4 2
◇ A 9 8 3
♣ 10 9 6 3

South (You)
♠ A Q 8 7 4
♡ K 6 3
◇ K
♣ A 8 4 2

Okay, you won this race, but can you win the one coming up?

EAST-WEST VUL.	DEALER NORTH		
West	**North**	**East**	**South**
	1♣	pass	1♠
pass	2♠	pass	2NT
pass	4♠	all pass	

North
♠ A J 6 5
♡ A 7 6
◇ 4
♣ K 7 6 4 3

South (Swifty)
♠ K 7 4 3
♡ K 5 3
◇ J 6 2
♣ A J 5

Against silent opposition you reach 4♠. West leads the ◇K and shifts smartly to the ♡10. Any big plans?

You've lost a diamond and you have possible losers in each of the other three suits, two of which have finesse possibilities. You really don't think this hand would be in here if it were right to take either finesse, do you? Right on. But what should you do?

Best is to win the ♡K, play the king and ace of spades, and assuming nothing traumatic has happened (4-1 spades*) and the ♠Q is still outstanding, play the king and ace of clubs followed by the jack! Have you gone stark raving mad? Have I? Hardly. Assuming clubs are 3-2, you have just established two club winners in dummy. Say someone wins and leads a heart (or even cashes the high trump and leads a heart). No problem. Win the ♡A, play a winning club from dummy and discard your losing heart. You can use your other club to discard a diamond and your odd diamond can be ruffed in dummy. Don't look now, but you have made 4♠ , losing one club, one spade, one diamond, no hearts, and no finesses!

Why abandon all these lovely looking finesses? Because you don't have time to take either one. Say you take the spade finesse; it loses, and a heart comes back. If the club finesse loses as well, you will lose a trick in every suit. What about the club finesse? No good either. If that loses and a heart comes back you may not have time to discard a heart on the fourth club; someone may ruff the third club. What you have to do is to set up the club suit for a heart discard without letting them in until the club suit is established. Take a look at a reasonable construction of the East-West hands and maybe you will see why it is incorrect to take either finesse. In fact, play it out if you are having trouble seeing this one.

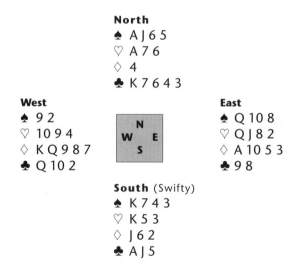

North
♠ A J 6 5
♡ A 7 6
♢ 4
♣ K 7 6 4 3

West
♠ 9 2
♡ 10 9 4
♢ K Q 9 8 7
♣ Q 10 2

East
♠ Q 10 8
♡ Q J 8 2
♢ A 10 5 3
♣ 9 8

South (Swifty)
♠ K 7 4 3
♡ K 5 3
♢ J 6 2
♣ A J 5

Common finesse combinations

Resisting temptation

It is helpful to recognize common card combinations that offer finesse possibilities. Not to disillusion you, but with this one it may be best not to finesse immediately.

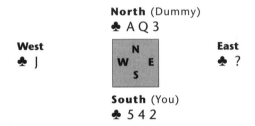

North (Dummy)
♣ A Q 3

West
♣ J

East
♣ ?

South (You)
♣ 5 4 2

Either in a suit contract or at notrump, the ♣ J is led and you have no clue who has the king. If you cannot afford to lose even one club trick, and you do have a place to park one of your baby clubs, take the finesse. But say you can afford to lose one club trick, but not two — and you are going to have to give up the lead (perhaps the ace of your long suit is missing). Consider the effect of playing the ace of clubs on this first trick! No, you haven't gone mad. If West has the ♣ K, your ♣ Q still takes a trick, only later. Many players have trouble seeing that. But when East has the ♣ K, the play of the ace can reap a huge gain. After the ace is played, if *East* is the next player to get the lead, East will not be able to attack clubs without surrendering a trick to dummy's queen. Are you beginning to see the possibilities?

North
♠ 7
♡ K Q 6 4
◇ 10 8 7 3 2
♣ A Q 5

West
♠ K J 8 4
♡ 10 8 7 2
◇ 4
♣ J 10 9 2

East
♠ Q 9 6 5 3
♡ A J 5 3
◇ Q
♣ K 8 6

South
♠ A 10 2
♡ 9
◇ A K J 9 6 5
♣ 7 4 3

NEITHER VUL.		DEALER SOUTH	
West	**North**	**East**	**South**
			1◇
pass	1♡	1♠	2◇
3♠[1]	5◇	all pass	

1. Preemptive.

West leads the ♣J, and with one loser in hearts, you see you can afford to lose one club trick, but not two. If you take the club finesse (the right play if the contract was 6◇) and it loses and a club is returned, you stand to lose two clubs and a heart; down one.

But what if you play the ♣A, draw trumps, and lead a heart? This loses, as it happens, to East's ace. East cannot continue clubs without establishing dummy's queen, and if East doesn't cash the ♣K, you can discard a club on a heart. But what if West has the ♡A and plays a club? You play the queen, of course. You are probably going down if East has the ♣K, but you are no worse off than if you had played the ♣Q at Trick 1 (see sidebar).

This next deal features a similar maneuver — the situation just comes up later in the play.

Actually, you are better off, because if East started with a doubleton ♣K, you are still going to make this hand, whereas you would have gone down by taking the finesse at Trick 1.

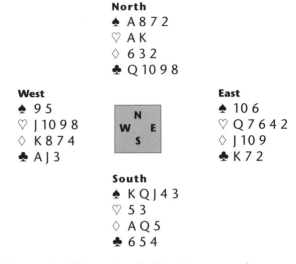

BOTH VUL.   DEALER NORTH

West	North	East	South
	1♣	pass	1♠
pass	2♠	pass	4♠
all pass			

North
♠ A 8 7 2
♡ A K
◇ 6 3 2
♣ Q 10 9 8

West
♠ 9 5
♡ J 10 9 8
◇ K 8 7 4
♣ A J 3

East
♠ 10 6
♡ Q 7 6 4 2
◇ J 10 9
♣ K 7 2

South
♠ K Q J 4 3
♡ 5 3
◇ A Q 5
♣ 6 5 4

You cleverly win the ♡J opening lead in dummy, cash two trumps ending in your hand, and lead a club to the ten and king, marking the ♣J with West — good thinking. East shifts to the ◇J and your moment of truth has arrived. If you finesse the queen, you are at the mercy of the ◇K. If the finesse loses and a diamond comes back, driving out the ace, the opponents may be able to take the setting trick in diamonds when they get in with the ♣A. However, if you rise with the ◇A and play another club to West's ace, your diamond ◇Q is protected, and you have time to discard a diamond on dummy's fourth club.

More traps

Three of the more commonly misplayed finesse combinations (by other players) are coming up:

1.

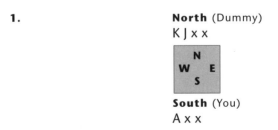

North (Dummy)
K J x x

South (You)
A x x

If you need *four* tricks, play West for Qxx. Cash the ace and then lead low to the jack, or just lead low to the jack. Don't hold your breath — West is going to have Qxx only 18% of the time.

However, if you just need *three* tricks, you can employ a safety play: low to the king, low to the ace, and only then low toward the jack. You have just improved your chances to 77%. Study the following diagram:

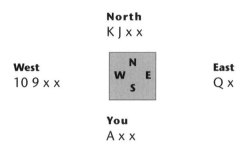

North
K J x x

West
10 9 x x

East
Q x

You
A x x

If you start with the king, then low to the ace, and then low to the jack, you take three tricks when East has a doubleton queen, but you also take three tricks any time West has the queen or the suit is divided 3-3.

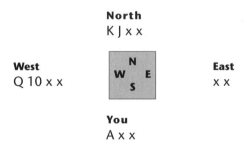

North
K J x x

West
Q 10 x x

East
x x

You
A x x

You lead low to the king, low to the ace, and then low towards the Jx in dummy. West has the Q10 left and might as well take the queen. But dummy's jack is now high and you have three tricks.

2.

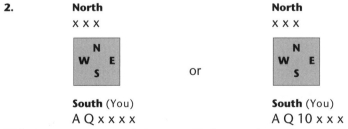

North
x x x

South (You)
A Q x x x

or

North
x x x

South (You)
A Q 10 x x x

This is your trump suit in a small slam and you have no other losers. In other words, you can afford to lose one trick, but not two. In order to take five tricks and cater to all possibilities, bang down the ace. If the king doesn't drop, enter dummy and lead up to the queen. As long as West didn't start with KJx, in which case you were always dead meat, you will take *five* tricks. The play of the ace guards against a singleton king in the West hand and costs nothing. Of course, if you need all six tricks, lead low to the queen.

3. Only players like you get this next one right.

North (Dummy)
x x x

West	**East**
a. K 9	a. J 10 8 7
b. 10 9	b. K J 8 7
c. 10 9 7	c. K J 8

South (You)
A Q x x

Again it depends upon how many tricks you need. If you need three tricks, you must find East with Kxx specifically — layout (c). Don't hold your breath, it's another 18% chance. The normal way of going about getting those three tricks is to start by playing low from both hands, then crossing to dummy and leading low to the queen.

However, if you need *two* tricks only, again start by playing low from both hands, but then cash the ace. If the king still hasn't appeared, cross to dummy and lead low to the queen. Let's see how it works, looking at some possible East-West holdings. Say you play low from both hands and then play the ace. In (a) the king drops so your queen is high. Now let's say nothing happens when you play the ace, so you cross to dummy and lead up to the queen. When East has the king — layouts (b) and (c) — the queen becomes your second trick.

Before attacking a suit with finesse possibilities, ask yourself how many tricks you need in the suit and then play accordingly. The bottom line is that you have to become familiar with the common card combinations.

Count your tricks!

Regardless of the lesson topic, it is assumed that you count your tricks before you begin the play (and during the play). It is the one sure guide that lets you avoid doing something stupid!

BOTH VUL.		DEALER SOUTH	
West	**North**	**East**	**South**
			2♣
pass	2◊	pass	2NT[1]
pass	6NT	all pass	

1. 22-24 HCP.

Opening lead: ♡Q

North (Dummy)
♠ A 6 5
♡ K 3 2
◊ Q 6 5
♣ K 10 8 2

South (You)
♠ K J 3 2
♡ A 6 4
◊ A K 7
♣ A Q J

You count nine tricks outside of spades, the suit you are planning to work with, so you need *three* spade tricks. Remember how to do that? Start with the ♠ K, then over to dummy's ♠ A, and finally low to your ♠ J. As it happens, careful play is rewarded. West turns out to have ♠ Qx, so you pick up the queen and make your slam. Had you finessed the ♠ J, you would have a little explaining to do after the hand.

Count your sure tricks outside of the suit you are planning to establish. This tells you how many tricks you need in your key suit. Now all you have to do is know how to play the suit for the required number of tricks!

NEITHER VUL.   DEALER WEST

West	North	East	South
1◇	pass	pass	2♡[1]
pass	4♡	all pass	

1. Intermediate in the 'balancing' seat.

North (Dummy)
♠ A Q 10 3
♡ Q 9 3 2
◇ Q J 5
♣ 7 6

West
♠ K J 8 7
♡ 6
◇ A K 9 3 2
♣ K 9 5

East
♠ 9 4 2
♡ 5 4
◇ 10 8
♣ Q 10 8 4 3 2

South (You)
♠ 6 5
♡ A K J 10 8 7
◇ 7 6 4
♣ A J

The opening lead is the ◇A (ace from AKx(x) at Trick 1). East signals high-low on the ace and king of diamonds, ruffs the third diamond, and switches to the ♣ 4 which you win with the ace. Where do you go from here?

Counting top tricks only, you have six hearts, one club, and one spade for eight. In other words, you need *two* additional tricks and they can only come from spades. The finesse of the ♠ Q, assuming it works, gives you one extra trick. Not enough. You have to go deeper; finesse the ♠ 10, and then the ♠ Q. You need to play West for both spade honors. Had you not counted the tricks you needed, you might have settled for leading a spade to the queen.

Test yourself

1.

North
♠ Q J 10 9
♡ A Q 9 2
◇ A 2
♣ 7 6 3

South (You)
♠ 7 6
♡ K J 10 8 7
◇ K 5
♣ A Q 5 4

NORTH-SOUTH VUL. DEALER SOUTH			
West	**North**	**East**	**South**
			1♡
pass	2NT[1]	pass	3♣[2]
pass	4♡[3]	all pass	

1.	13-15 balanced, but might contain 4-card support (not Jacoby).
2.	Natural.
3.	Confirming 4-card support.

You play 4♡, and the lead is the ◇Q. You win in dummy, draw trumps in two rounds, and lead the ♠Q from dummy. East wins the ♠ A and shifts to the ♣ 10. Plan the play.

Solution on page 113

2.

North
♠ 10 9 8 6
♡ K 6 2
◇ Q J
♣ A 7 4 2

South (You)
♠ A Q J 5 4
♡ A 5 4
◇ K 7 4
♣ Q J

NEITHER VUL. DEALER SOUTH			
West	**North**	**East**	**South**
			1♠
pass	3♠[1]	pass	4♠
all pass			

1.	Isn't it lovely to always have four-card support?

West leads the ♡J against 4♠. Plan the play.

Solution on page 113

EAST-WEST VUL.   DEALER SOUTH

West	North	East	South
			1♢
pass	2NT[1]	pass	3♣
pass	3NT	pass	4♢
pass	4♡[2]	pass	4NT[3]
pass	5♡[4]	pass	5NT
pass	7♢[5]	all pass	

1. 13-15 HCP.
2. Cuebid.
3. Regular Blackwood.
4. Two aces.
5. Needing a big swing to win the match and afraid to bid 7NT.

Solution on page 114

NEITHER VUL.   DEALER SOUTH

West	North	East	South
			2NT
pass	6NT	all pass	

Solution on page 115

3.

North
♠ A Q J
♡ A Q 5
♢ J 8 7 6
♣ 7 6 5

South
♠ 6 4
♡ 8 2
♢ A K Q 10 5 4
♣ A K Q

Your partner's insecurities have landed you in a grand slam from the wrong side. West, a tricky player, leads the ♡4. Can you make partner's bidding look good?

4.

North
♠ J 7
♡ A 6 2
♢ A K 10 5 3
♣ 6 4 2

South (You)
♠ A K 4 2
♡ K Q 3
♢ Q J 8
♣ A Q 7

West leads the ♡J against 6NT. Plan the play.

5.

North
♠ 3 2
♡ A 9 7 6 4
◇ Q J 10
♣ A K 2

South (You)
♠ A K Q J 9 7 4
♡ K 3
◇ A 6
♣ 7 3

BOTH VUL.		DEALER SOUTH	
West	**North**	**East**	**South**
			1♠
pass	2♡	pass	3♠
pass	4♣[1]	pass	4NT[2]
pass	5♡[3]	pass	5NT[4]
pass	6♣[5]	pass	7♠[6]
all pass			

1.	Cuebid.
2.	RKB.
3.	Two.
4.	Specific kings?
5.	♣K.
6.	Planning on setting up dummy's hearts for a diamond pitch.

Unimpressed with all these club cuebids, West leads the ♣J. Plan the play.

Solution on page 116

6.

North
♠ A 6 2
♡ K J 8 4 2
◇ Q 8 6
♣ 7 2

South (You)
♠ K J 3
♡ A Q 10 9 7
◇ J 4 2
♣ A K

NEITHER VUL.		DEALER SOUTH	
West	**North**	**East**	**South**
			1♡
pass	3♡[1]	pass	4♡[2]
all pass			

1.	Limit raise.
2.	Facing a limit raise don't even think about a slam, unless you have a singleton or a void, and a big hand.

You are declarer in 4♡ on the lead of the ♣Q. Plan the play.

Solution on page 117

7.

NEITHER VUL.		DEALER WEST	
West	**North**	**East**	**South**
		pass	1◇
pass	2♣	pass	2◇
pass	3◇	pass	3♡
pass	4♣[1]	pass	5◇
all pass			

1.   Cuebid.

North
♠ 4 2
♡ J 10
◇ K 9 6 5
♣ A K 10 3 2

South (You)
♠ 10 7
♡ A Q 6
◇ A Q J 10 3
♣ J 9 5

Solution on page 118

With a keen ear for the bidding, West leads the ♠K against your 5◇ game. East plays an encouraging spade and West continues with a low spade to East's ace. East shifts to the inevitable low heart. Now it's up to you.

8.

BOTH VUL.		DEALER SOUTH	
West	**North**	**East**	**South**
			1♡
1♠	4♡	4♠	6♡
all pass			

North
♠ —
♡ Q J 9 8 6 5
◇ Q 10 9 8
♣ 9 6 2

South (You)
♠ Q J 8 6
♡ A K 10 7 3 2
◇ —
♣ A Q 5

Solution on page 119

The opening lead is the ♠3. Plan the play.

9.

North
♠ A J 5 4
♡ J 8 3
◇ K Q 10 8
♣ 6 3

South (You)
♠ K 10 6 3
♡ Q 5 4
◇ A J 3 2
♣ A K

| EAST-WEST VUL. | | DEALER SOUTH | |
West	**North**	**East**	**South**
			1NT
pass	2♣	pass	2♠
pass	4♠	all pass	

After you open 1NT, partner Staymans you into 4♠. West leads a low club and East plays the queen. Assuming spades are 3-2, who do you play for the trump queen? Plan the play.

Solution on page 120

For the next four questions, assume you are South, dummy is North, and you have plenty of back and forth entries in the other suits. Answer the questions following each diagram:

10.

North (Dummy)
x x x

South (You)
A Q 10 x x x

a) What is the best play for six tricks?
b) For five tricks?

Solutions on page 120

11.

North (Dummy)
K J x x

South (You)
A x x

a) What is the best play for four tricks?
b) For three tricks?

Solutions on page 120

12.

North (Dummy)
x x

South (You)
A Q x x x x x

a) What is the best play for seven tricks?

Solutions on page 120

b) For six tricks?

13.

North (Dummy)
A Q x x

South (You)
x x x

a) What is the best play for three tricks?

Solutions on page 120

b) For two tricks?

Test yourself — solutions

1.

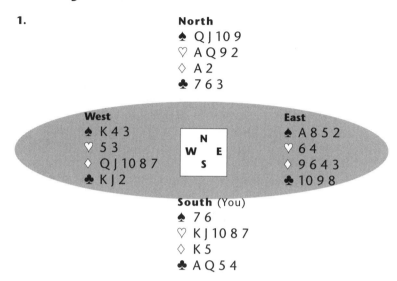

North
♠ Q J 10 9
♡ A Q 9 2
◇ A 2
♣ 7 6 3

West
♠ K 4 3
♡ 5 3
◇ Q J 10 8 7
♣ K J 2

East
♠ A 8 5 2
♡ 6 4
◇ 9 6 4 3
♣ 10 9 8

South (You)
♠ 7 6
♡ K J 10 8 7
◇ K 5
♣ A Q 5 4

NORTH-SOUTH VUL. DEALER SOUTH

West	North	East	South
			1♡
pass	2NT[1]	pass	3♣[2]
pass	4♡[3]	all pass	

1. 13-15 balanced, but might contain 4-card support (not Jacoby).
2. Natural.
3. Confirming 4-card support.

Trick 1: ◇Q ◇A ◇4 ◇5
Trick 2: ♡4 ♡2 ♡K ♡3
Trick 3: ♡7 ♡5 ♡A ♡6
Trick 4: ♠Q ♠A ♠6 ♠3
Trick 5: ♣10 ?

The idea is to try to get rid of two clubs on dummy's spades while losing one club and two spades max. In order to do this, rise with the ♣ A, the key play, cash the ◇K, and lead a second spade. If West wins, you are 100% safe. You can eventually discard two clubs on dummy's spades, losing one club and two spades. If East wins and returns a club, play the queen. You still survive if East has the ♣ K or if West has a doubleton king (since West will be endplayed upon winning the trick). If you finesse the ♣ Q at Trick 5 (for shame), and West wins and returns a club, you go down if the player with the ♠ K has a club.

2.

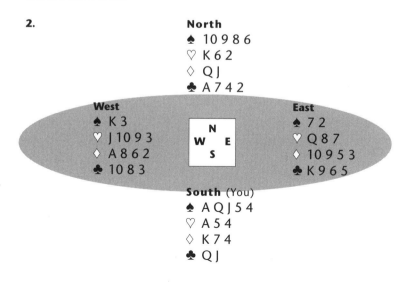

North
♠ 10 9 8 6
♡ K 6 2
◇ Q J
♣ A 7 4 2

West
♠ K 3
♡ J 10 9 3
◇ A 8 6 2
♣ 10 8 3

East
♠ 7 2
♡ Q 8 7
◇ 10 9 5 3
♣ K 9 6 5

South (You)
♠ A Q J 5 4
♡ A 5 4
◇ K 7 4
♣ Q J

NEITHER VUL.   DEALER SOUTH

West	North	East	South
			1♠
pass	3♠	pass	4♠
all pass			

Opening lead: ♡J

You are faced with a possible loser in each suit, and finesse possibilities in two suits. Stay calm!

The first order of business is to dispose of that heart loser; the rest can wait. If you can get rid of the heart loser, it won't matter if both black suit finesses fail. Win the ♡K in dummy and lead a diamond honor. Best defense is for someone to win and play a second heart. Win the ♡A, cross to a diamond in dummy, return to the ♠A (don't even think of finessing!) and discard dummy's losing heart on your ◇K. Once that heart loser is history, drive out the ♠K and eventually take the club finesse going for a safe overtrick.

If you greedily take either black suit finesse before knocking out the ◇A, down you go. Say you take the spade finesse at Trick 2, it loses, and a heart comes back. Now you don't have time to set up your diamonds as the opponents have already set up a heart winner. Now you are reduced to the club finesse to make your contract. If you win the opening lead in your hand and try the club finesse, you will also be in trouble if it loses. Say a heart comes back. You win and unblock the ♣J, but you can't get to dummy to discard a heart on the ♣A without letting the opponents in to cash a heart. Pity.

Basically, you have to ask yourself tough questions before you embark on a line of play, like, 'What can happen to me if I take the club (spade) finesse and it loses?' Once you see the danger, you might realize diamonds are your salvation.

3.

EAST-WEST VUL.	DEALER SOUTH		
West	**North**	**East**	**South**
			1◇
pass	2NT[1]	pass	3♣
pass	3NT	pass	4◇
pass	4♡[2]	pass	4NT[3]
pass	5♡[4]	pass	5NT
pass	7◇[5]	all pass	

1. 13-15 HCP.
2. Cuebid.
3. Regular Blackwood.
4. Two aces.
5. Madness.

Opening lead: ♡4

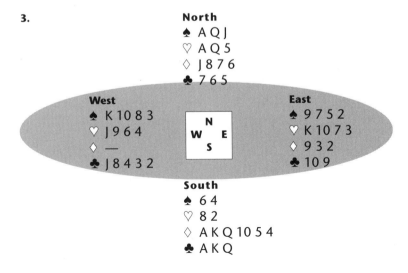

North
♠ A Q J
♡ A Q 5
◇ J 8 7 6
♣ 7 6 5

West
♠ K 10 8 3
♡ J 9 6 4
◇ —
♣ J 8 4 3 2

East
♠ 9 7 5 2
♡ K 10 7 3
◇ 9 3 2
♣ 10 9

South
♠ 6 4
♡ 8 2
◇ A K Q 10 5 4
♣ A K Q

Don't tell me you went for that garbage about West being a tricky player — the heart finesse is a practice finesse! *Even if it works, you need the spade finesse.* But if the spade finesse works, it can be repeated, and you won't need the heart finesse. Why take two finesses when one is all you need? Rise with the ace of hearts, draw trump, and finesse the spade. If it works, return to your hand and repeat the finesse.

4.

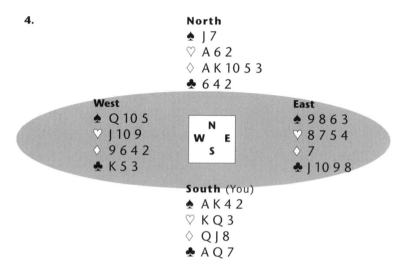

North
♠ J 7
♡ A 6 2
◇ A K 10 5 3
♣ 6 4 2

West
♠ Q 10 5
♡ J 10 9
◇ 9 6 4 2
♣ K 5 3

East
♠ 9 8 6 3
♡ 8 7 5 4
◇ 7
♣ J 10 9 8

South (You)
♠ A K 4 2
♡ K Q 3
◇ Q J 8
♣ A Q 7

NEITHER VUL.		DEALER SOUTH	
West	North	East	South
			2NT
pass	6NT	all pass	

Opening lead: ♡J

You start with eleven top tricks and have two chances for a twelfth — the club finesse might work (not in this book, of course!) or West may have the ♠ Q, in which case you can lead a low spade to the jack and garner your twelfth trick that way. In order to give yourself two chances, start by leading a low spade from your hand; if the jack loses to the queen, fall back on the club finesse. If you take the club finesse first and it loses, you no longer have the luxury of leading a low spade to the jack. In general, attacking unevenly divided suits takes prededence over attacking evenly divided suits; there is no chance for length establishment in evenly divided suits.

BOTH VUL.　　　DEALER SOUTH

West	North	East	South
			1♠
pass	2♡	pass	3♠
pass	4♣[1]	pass	4NT[2]
pass	5♡[3]	pass	5NT[4]
pass	6♣[5]	pass	7♠[6]
all pass			

1.　Cuebid.
2.　RKB.
3.　Two.
4.　Specific kings?
5.　♣K.
6.　Planning to establish dummy's hearts for a diamond pitch.

Opening lead: ♣J

5.

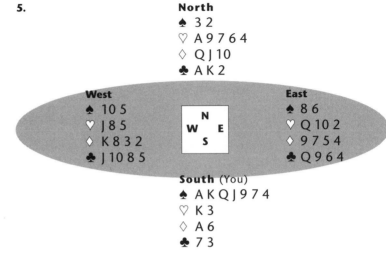

North
♠ 3 2
♡ A 9 7 6 4
◇ Q J 10
♣ A K 2

West
♠ 10 5
♡ J 8 5
◇ K 8 3 2
♣ J 10 8 5

East
♠ 8 6
♡ Q 10 2
◇ 9 7 5 4
♣ Q 9 6 4

South (You)
♠ A K Q J 9 7 4
♡ K 3
◇ A 6
♣ 7 3

The idea, as ever, is to give yourself two chances. In other words, don't put all your eggs in the diamond finesse basket; test hearts first. If hearts are 3-3, you won't need the diamond finesse. After winning the opening lead, draw trumps and play the king — ace and ruff a heart. If hearts are 3-3, your diamond loser goes off on one of dummy's two good hearts. If hearts are not 3-3, take the diamond finesse. Two chances are better than one.

6.

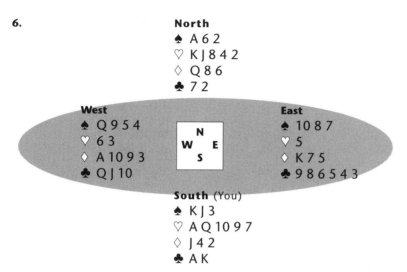

North
♠ A 6 2
♡ K J 8 4 2
◊ Q 8 6
♣ 7 2

West
♠ Q 9 5 4
♡ 6 3
◊ A 10 9 3
♣ Q J 10

East
♠ 10 8 7
♡ 5
◊ K 7 5
♣ 9 8 6 5 4 3

South (You)
♠ K J 3
♡ A Q 10 9 7
◊ J 4 2
♣ A K

NEITHER VUL.   DEALER SOUTH

West	North	East	South
			1♡
pass	3♡[1]	pass	4♡[2]
all pass			

1. Limit raise.
2. Facing a limit raise don't even think about a slam, unless you have a singleton or a void and a big hand.

A perfect example of when not to finesse. You have a touchy diamond suit that you would rather the opponents lead to you. If you can force a diamond lead from either opponent you can lose no more than two diamond tricks. If you use your equal length spade suit as your throw-in suit, that wish will come true.

Draw trumps, cash both your clubs, and play the ace, king and jack of spades (treating the jack of spades with a bit of contempt, as if it were a small card). Whoever wins must lead a diamond (or give you a ruff and a sluff). The most you can lose is one spade and two diamonds. If you take the spade finesse (a practice finesse if there ever was one) and it loses, a spade can be returned and now you have to attack diamonds yourself. Not healthy.

7.

E-W VUL.		DEALER EAST	
West	**North**	**East**	**South**
		pass	1◇
pass	2♣	pass	2◇
pass	3◇	pass	3♡
pass	4♣[1]	pass	5◇
all pass			

1. Cuebid.

Trick 1: ♠K ♠2 ♠8 ♠7
Trick 2: ♠3 ♠4 ♠A ♠10
Trick 3: ♡3 ?

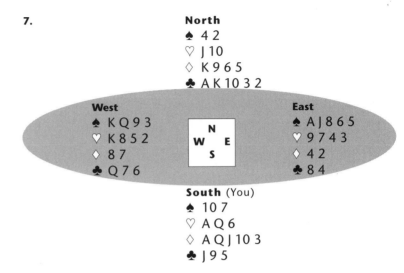

North
♠ 4 2
♡ J 10
◇ K 9 6 5
♣ A K 10 3 2

West
♠ K Q 9 3
♡ K 8 5 2
◇ 8 7
♣ Q 7 6

East
♠ A J 8 6 5
♡ 9 7 4 3
◇ 4 2
♣ 8 4

South (You)
♠ 10 7
♡ A Q 6
◇ A Q J 10 3
♣ J 9 5

Do not take the heart finesse! Even if it works, you still need the club finesse. But if the club finesse works, you can discard both hearts on the clubs. Why take two finesses when one will do? Win the ace of hearts, play a club to the ace, draw trumps ending in your hand, and run the ♣ J. If the finesse works, you make your contract; if it doesn't, you go down two. *C'est la vie.* But the heart finesse is strictly cosmetic.

8.

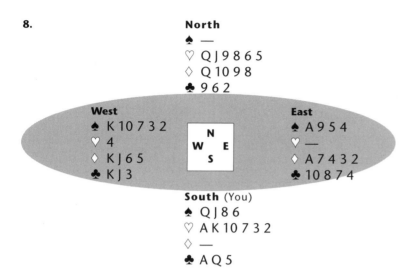

North
♠ —
♡ Q J 9 8 6 5
◇ Q 10 9 8
♣ 9 6 2

West
♠ K 10 7 3 2
♡ 4
◇ K J 6 5
♣ K J 3

East
♠ A 9 5 4
♡ —
◇ A 7 4 3 2
♣ 10 8 7 4

South (You)
♠ Q J 8 6
♡ A K 10 7 3 2
◇ —
♣ A Q 5

BOTH VUL.   DEALER SOUTH

West	North	East	South
			1♡
1♠	4♡	4♠	6♡
all pass			

Opening lead: ♠3

The spade honors figure to be split on the bidding and the lead of a
low card normally promises an honor. If so, you can discard a club
from dummy on the opening lead, allowing East to win the trick,
surely with the ace. Win the club return with the ace, draw the outstanding trumps, and run the ♠Q through West. Assuming West
has the ♠K, you will be able to pitch dummy's remaining club on
the established ♠J. If West doesn't cover, discard dummy's last club.
All you are doing is playing West, the original overcaller, for the ♠K.
This must be better than playing East for the ♣K.

9.

EAST-WEST VUL.   DEALER SOUTH

West	North	East	South
			1NT
pass	2♣	pass	2♠
pass	4♠	all pass	

Trick 1: ♣2 ♣3 ♣Q ♣A
Trick 2: ?

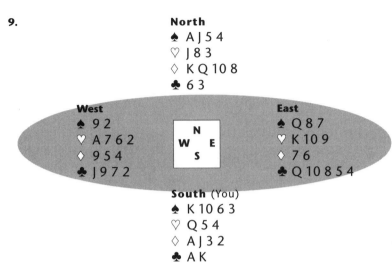

North
♠ A J 5 4
♡ J 8 3
◊ K Q 10 8
♣ 6 3

West
♠ 9 2
♡ A 7 6 2
◊ 9 5 4
♣ J 9 7 2

East
♠ Q 8 7
♡ K 10 9
◊ 7 6
♣ Q 10 8 5 4

South (You)
♠ K 10 6 3
♡ Q 5 4
◊ A J 3 2
♣ A K

It doesn't matter who has the spade queen! You have three likely heart losers (unless they lead the suit) and a possible spade loser. Use your likely trump loser to force the opponents to make a heart play. At Tricks 2 and 3 play the ace and king of spades, giving up on the trump finesse, presumably leaving the queen at large. Next cash out your clubs and then your diamonds. If nobody ruffs, exit a trump. The opponent on lead will either have to break hearts or give you a ruff and a sluff. Either way you lose only two more tricks.

10. a) Lead low to the queen hoping that RHO has Kx or LHO a singleton jack. In the latter case, return to dummy and lead low to the ten.
b) Lead the ace, guarding against a singleton king on your left. If the king doesn't drop, enter dummy and lead low toward your hand. Unless your LHO has both missing honors, you cannot lose more than one trick.

11. a) Lead the ace and low to the jack, or low to the jack. You must find LHO with Qxx.
b) Play the king, then low to the ace, then low to the jack guarding against Qx on your right. You will still take three tricks if the suit divides 3-3 or the queen is to your left.

12. a) Lead low to the queen, hoping RHO has Kx specifically.
b) Play the ace in case LHO has a stiff king; if not, enter dummy and lead low to the queen.

13. a) Play low from both hands, starting from the dummy, and then lead low from your hand to the queen in dummy; you must find LHO with Kxx specifically or RHO making a blunder with Kxx.

b) Play low from both hands starting from dummy, then cash the ace, and if the king has not appeared, enter your hand and lead low towards the queen. You win any time either player has a singleton or doubleton king, or the suit breaks 3-3, or whenever LHO has the king, or whenever RHO blunders with something like K10xx.

Key ideas from Chapter 3

- Although finesses, particularly in long suits, play a big part in the game, if a finesse can be avoided in favor of a safer play, go for it.
- There are many techniques available to help you avoid or postpone finesses:

  a) Trying to set up a long suit first.

  b) When two finesses are available, taking the one that will make the other unnecessary.

  c) Using a side suit that has finesse possibilities, if equally divided, as a **throw-in suit** to force the opponents to lead another suit.

  d) **Ruffing out** a missing honor in one suit before taking a finesse in another.

  e) Using your trump suit as a throw-in suit rather than taking a trump finesse.

  f) **Discarding** a loser from dummy when dummy is void in the suit that has been led, and you have Kx(x), KQx(x), QJx(x), etc.

  g) Playing the ace from an AQx(x) combination when an opponent leads through the suit in order to **preserve a stopper** in case the king lies over the queen.

When to Finesse (Finally)

A lucky chance that oft decides the fate of mighty monarchs.

JAMES THOMPSON

The previous chapter dealt with avoiding finesses; this one deals with taking them, but taking them at the proper time, in the proper order and aiming them into the proper hand, if possible. It also deals with leading the proper card when taking a finesse. There is more to finessing than meets the eye.

The element of time

There is quite a difference between planning a finesse to avoid an immediate loser or two, as opposed to taking a finesse to rid yourself of an eventual loser that is still protected by an ace. The 'urgency' factor comes into play. Let's look at an example:

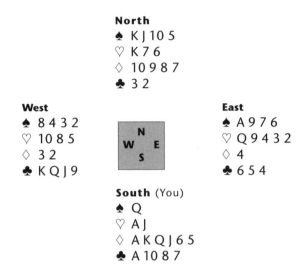

North
♠ K J 10 5
♡ K 7 6
♢ 10 9 8 7
♣ 3 2

West
♠ 8 4 3 2
♡ 10 8 5
♢ 3 2
♣ K Q J 9

East
♠ A 9 7 6
♡ Q 9 4 3 2
♢ 4
♣ 6 5 4

South (You)
♠ Q
♡ A J
♢ A K Q J 6 5
♣ A 10 8 7

You arrive at a contract of six diamonds, and West leads the club king. What are your thoughts?

With that %$&# club lead you do not have *time* to establish dummy's spades for club discards. Now your only chance is to enter dummy with a trump and take the heart finesse in an effort to get rid of your spade. Assuming it works, cash the ♡A, re-enter dummy with a trump, discard the ♠Q on the ♡K, concede a club and claim.

When you do not have time to set up a suit for discards, you may be forced to take a finesse in a no-loser suit to generate an extra winner.

Finesses in the trump suit

More often than not, the trump suit should be attacked early. There may be a two-way finesse for a queen, and one can get lost in nursery rhymes — 'eight ever, nine never,' etc.

The trick to playing most contracts is to consider the hand as an entire unit, rather than concentrating on just one suit. For example, in addition to a possible trump suit problem, there may be a side suit that you don't want led from a particular opponent, the **danger hand**. It is important to take finesses through, not into the danger hand.

North
♠ K 9 5 3
♡ 7 5 3
♢ A Q J 6
♣ A 2

```
   N
 W   E
   S
```

South (You)
♠ A J 10 8 7
♡ K 4 2
♢ K 10 7
♣ K 3

		BOTH VUL.	DEALER NORTH
West	**North**	**East**	**South**
	1♢	pass	1♠
pass	2♠	pass	4♠
all pass			

Opening Lead: ♣Q

When you look at these hands, what should you see? You should see a trump suit missing the queen, a heart suit that is vulnerable to attack from East and a diamond suit that can furnish a discard, preferably after trumps have been drawn; in addition, you have a no-loser club suit. The idea is to coordinate the play to take advantage of all your pluses.

Since East is the danger hand, take the spade finesse into West. Win the first trick with the ♣K, try the effect of playing the ♠J to the king (who knows, maybe West will cover...) and run the ♠9. So what if West wins the spade queen? Your ♡K is safe and one of your hearts is going away on dummy's fourth diamond.

The full deal:

North
♠ K 9 5 3
♡ 7 5 3
♢ A Q J 6
♣ A 2

West
♠ 6
♡ A 8 6
♢ 9 8 5 4
♣ Q J 10 9 4

```
   N
 W   E
   S
```

East
♠ Q 4 2
♡ Q J 10 9
♢ 3 2
♣ 8 7 6 5

South
♠ A J 10 8 7
♡ K 4 2
♢ K 10 7
♣ K 3

When you have a two-way finesse for a queen, plus another suit that is vulnerable to attack from one opponent only (the danger hand), aim your two-way finesses through the danger hand into the non-danger hand.

Two-way finesses in the side suits

Two-way finesses are not confined to the trump suit. Once you isolate a danger hand, go out of your way to take *all* finesses into the other hand.

NORTH-SOUTH VUL. DEALER WEST

West	North	East	South
2♠	dbl	pass	3NT
all pass			

North
♠ 3 2
♡ A J 8 5
◇ A J 10 4 3
♣ A 10

South (You)
♠ K J 9
♡ K 3
◇ K 9 5 2
♣ K 6 5 3

West opens 2♠, weak, partner doubles, and your 3NT response ends the auction. Undaunted, West leads the ♠7, East produces the ♠10, and you win the ♠J. Now what?

Outside of your main suit, diamonds, you have five sure tricks: the spade you have just taken plus the aces and kings of hearts and clubs. In other words, you only need four diamond tricks, not five, to make this hand.

Equally important is the positional factor of your present spade stopper. If West gets the lead, you retain a spade stopper, but if East gets the lead, a spade through your K-9 will ruin your whole day. You stand to lose five spade tricks if that happens. East is the danger hand — *Danger! Stay away!*

Fortunately your diamonds are so strong that you can keep East off lead regardless. Lead a diamond to the ace and run the ◊J. Either the finesse wins (in which case you are playing for overtricks), or the finesse loses leaving you with nine tricks plus a spade stopper that is still intact.

With a two-way finesse, plus a 'danger' hand, finesse through the danger hand into the non-danger hand.

The full deal:

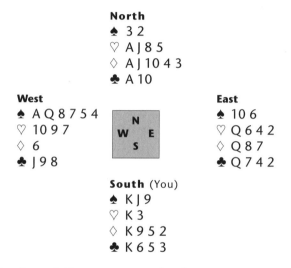

North
♠ 3 2
♡ A J 8 5
◊ A J 10 4 3
♣ A 10

West
♠ A Q 8 7 5 4
♡ 10 9 7
◊ 6
♣ J 9 8

East
♠ 10 6
♡ Q 6 4 2
◊ Q 8 7
♣ Q 7 4 2

South (You)
♠ K J 9
♡ K 3
◊ K 9 5 2
♣ K 6 5 3

So far, it has been fairly easy to spot the dangerous opponent, but sometimes it isn't quite that easy. Be careful: danger can lurk in unexpected places.

NEITHER VUL.		DEALER SOUTH	
West	**North**	**East**	**South**
			1NT
pass	2♣	pass	2◇
pass	3NT	all pass	

Opening lead: ♠ J

North

♠ K 7
♡ K 4 3 2
◇ J 6
♣ K 10 8 4 3

South (You)

♠ A Q 2
♡ 7 5
◇ A K 3 2
♣ A 9 5 2

The fact that you have received a seemingly favorable lead does not mean you should take your eye off the ball. You are still vulnerable in hearts, and your plan should revolve around keeping West, the player who might be able to hurt you with a heart switch, off play. This may not always be possible, but nevertheless you should give it the old college try.

With five winners outside of clubs, your main suit, you need only play clubs for four tricks, *but you must try to keep West off lead in the process.* When you are missing both the queen and jack in your main suit, but are blessed with the AK109 between the two hands, your chances are pretty good.

With a 4-4 or 5-4 fit, including the AK109, ace and king divided, you have all the makings of an avoidance finesse. Determine the danger hand, then aim your finesses the other way. The trick is to make sure that the danger hand plays *second* to the trick when finessing.

After winning the spade lead in your hand, start with a low club. If an honor appears from West, win the king and lead back to the ace. If East has Qxx you are still okay as you can afford to lose a club to East. If West plays a low card, stick in the eight. East wins, but you are safe. Even if East started with QJxx, you lose only one club trick. If you play carelessly, you could have an 'accident'. Say you bang down the ace-king of clubs and find West started with ♣ Qxx or ♣ Jxx. Now you have to let West in and run the risk of a heart shift. Don't look at me, I tried to warn you.

The full deal:

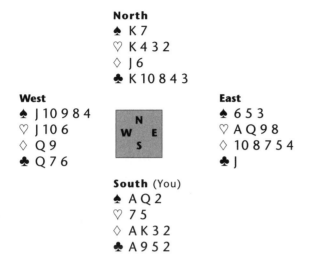

North
♠ K 7
♡ K 4 3 2
◇ J 6
♣ K 10 8 4 3

West
♠ J 10 9 8 4
♡ J 10 6
◇ Q 9
♣ Q 7 6

East
♠ 6 5 3
♡ A Q 9 8
◇ 10 8 7 5 4
♣ J

South (You)
♠ A Q 2
♡ 7 5
◇ A K 3 2
♣ A 9 5 2

Sometimes, the location of the danger hand may depend on your play to the first two or three tricks.

North
♠ 3 2
♡ A 7 5
◇ A J 10 8 6
♣ A 4 3

South (You)
♠ A J 9
♡ K 6 2
◇ Q 9 5 2
♣ K 7 6

BOTH VUL.		DEALER NORTH	
West	**North**	**East**	**South**
	1◇	pass	2NT
pass	3NT	all pass	

Opening Lead: ♠7

East plays the ♠K. Plan the play.

As things stand, if you win the first trick, East is the danger hand, because East can ram a spade through your J-9 with unhappy results — you know from the Rule of Eleven that West has led from the Q1087(x). However, if you duck the first two spades and win the third, suddenly West becomes the danger hand, because only West has winning spades (unless the suit was originally split 4-4, in which case you don't have a spade problem any more). In other words, you can control who you want to be the danger hand!

The key to the play is the direction that your diamond finesse is heading. The diamond finesse goes one way only, smack into East. Therefore, in order to extract East's fangs (his remaining spades), win the *third* spade and then finesse the diamond into East. Even if it loses, you are safe.

The full deal:

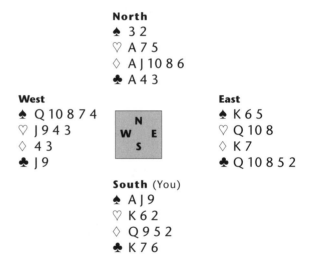

North
♠ 3 2
♡ A 7 5
◇ A J 10 8 6
♣ A 4 3

West
♠ Q 10 8 7 4
♡ J 9 4 3
◇ 4 3
♣ J 9

East
♠ K 6 5
♡ Q 10 8
◇ K 7
♣ Q 10 8 5 2

South (You)
♠ A J 9
♡ K 6 2
◇ Q 9 5 2
♣ K 7 6

Exchange the ◇A and ◇Q in the North-South hands and now the diamond finesse heads into West. Since you have a spade stopper if you win the ace and West later gets the lead, win the ♠A, cross to dummy and take the diamond finesse into West.

If you have a one-way finesse (for a king), if possible try to arrange that the opponent who might win the trick is the non-danger hand. A hold-up play prior to a finesse is one way to pull this off.

Length attracts shortness; shortness attracts length

This is sort of like the old saw, 'opposites attract'. Here's what it means in a bridge context. During the bidding you may discover that one opponent has a very long suit — a preemptive bidder, for example. You may know from the bidding that one hand has a seven-card suit while the partner has a doubleton in that suit. The player with the seven-card suit has six other cards, while the one with the doubleton has eleven other cards. It stands to reason that any missing card is almost twice as likely to be in the hand with the doubleton. Let's see how you can apply this in actual play.

North
♠ 8 5 4
♡ K J 3
♢ A 6 5
♣ A 7 5 4

South (You)
♠ Q J
♡ A 10 9 8 7 6
♢ K 4
♣ K 6 3

NEITHER VUL.		DEALER EAST	
West	**North**	**East**	**South**
		pass	1♡
2♠[1]	3♡	pass	4♡
all pass			

1.   Weak

Opening Lead: ♠A

West continues with the ♠K and ♠10; you ruff as East discards a diamond on the third spade. With a certain club loser, you have to avoid a trump loser. What should you do?

With no bidding to guide you, you would make the normal play in hearts: the ten to the king and the jack to the ace, playing for a 2-2 division. Notice that you have given each opponent a chance to cover an honor with an honor (a religious obligation to some, a moral obligation to others). But when one opponent has shown a long suit, it alters the odds of how to play other suits. *Reread that.* When the difference in length in a side suit (spades on this hand) is three or more cards, the percentages dictate playing the hand short in spades for length in the other suits. Lead a heart to the king and run the ♡J.

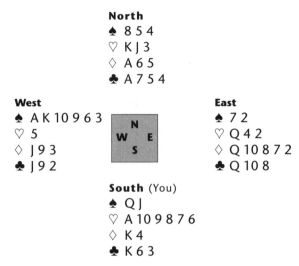

North
♠ 8 5 4
♡ K J 3
◇ A 6 5
♣ A 7 5 4

West
♠ A K 10 9 6 3
♡ 5
◇ J 9 3
♣ J 9 2

East
♠ 7 2
♡ Q 4 2
◇ Q 10 8 7 2
♣ Q 10 8

South (You)
♠ Q J
♡ A 10 9 8 7 6
◇ K 4
♣ K 6 3

In general, when one opponent is known to have three (or more) cards in one suit more than his partner, play the shorter hand for any missing jack or queen in another suit. (The exception to this is when the bidding tells you otherwise. The player with length may need the missing honor to justify his or her bidding.)

Choices

What should you do when you have two (or three) possible finesses to take and you need to take the right one to make your contract? Read on.

West	North	East	South
NEITHER VUL.		DEALER SOUTH	
			1NT
pass	2♣	pass	2◇
pass	3NT	all pass	

North
♠ K 5
♡ A J 7 2
◇ 10 9 2
♣ A Q 7 3

South (You)
♠ Q 6
♡ K 4 3
◇ A K J 4 3
♣ K 8 5

After you open 1NT, partner uses Stayman, and you arrive in 3NT. West leads the ♠3, you try the ♠K from dummy but East wins the

♠A and returns the ♠7 to your queen and West's deuce. So there you are. You have eight sure tricks (one spade, three clubs, two hearts, and two diamonds) and chances for an extra trick(s) in three suits. On the other hand, you can't let them in with all those spades loose out there. What should the order of plays be? Decide before reading on.

Clearly, the safest suit to attack is clubs. If clubs are 3-3, you have a ninth trick without risking a finesse. Say you test the clubs and West turns up with four clubs, East discarding a heart on the third round.

Now you are reduced to hearts and diamonds and you can take a finesse in either suit, but which? For such dilemmas the rule of 'extra chances' comes in handy:

The Rule of Extra Chances: *faced with a choice of finesses in two suits, each missing the queen, and not being able to let either opponent in, play the ace-king of the longer suit (diamonds in this example), and if the queen does not drop, take the finesse in the shorter suit (hearts in this case).*

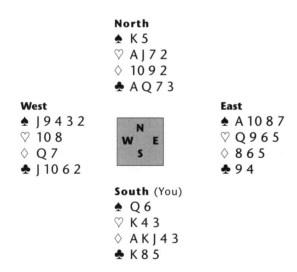

North
♠ K 5
♡ A J 7 2
♢ 10 9 2
♣ A Q 7 3

West
♠ J 9 4 3 2
♡ 10 8
♢ Q 7
♣ J 10 6 2

East
♠ A 10 8 7
♡ Q 9 6 5
♢ 8 6 5
♣ 9 4

South (You)
♠ Q 6
♡ K 4 3
♢ A K J 4 3
♣ K 8 5

In this case, I have sneakily set up a deal where if you take either finesse, you go down! But if you follow the Rule, and cash the two top diamonds first, guess what? The queen drops and you are home!

The Rule of Extra Chances can also be applied to contracts where you are missing a queen in one suit, a king in another, and have no margin for error (you can't let them in). Look at this next example:

North
♠ A J 7
♡ K 10 7
◇ 7 6
♣ Q 10 7 6 3

	N	
W		E
	S	

South (You)
♠ K 10 9 8
♡ A Q 2
◇ K 10
♣ A J 9 2

EAST-WEST VUL. DEALER SOUTH

West	North	East	South
			1NT
pass	3NT	all pass	

After a simple 1NT-3NT auction, West leads the ◇3 to East's ace, and East returns the ◇4 to your ◇K and West's ◇2.

You have seven top tricks: one diamond, two spades, three hearts and one club. Yet, if either the spade or the club finesse works, you make your contract easily, but which finesse should you take? After all, if you take the wrong one, diamond winners will come raining down upon you!

Give yourself two chances. Why put all of your eggs in one basket? Lead the ♠10 to the ♠A and the ♠J to the ♠K. Again, maybe someone will cover an honor with an honor even though you have no intention of finessing. If someone covers, or if the ♠Q drops doubleton, you have two extra spade tricks, or nine in all. If the queen does not drop, enter dummy with a heart and run the ♣Q.

North
♠ A J 7
♡ K 10 7
◇ 7 6
♣ Q 10 7 6 3

West
♠ Q 6
♡ 8 6 5
◇ Q J 8 3 2
♣ K 8 4

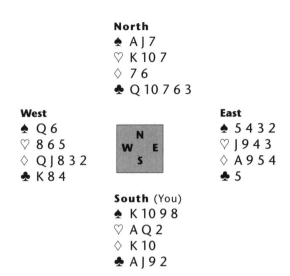

East
♠ 5 4 3 2
♡ J 9 4 3
◇ A 9 5 4
♣ 5

South (You)
♠ K 10 9 8
♡ A Q 2
◇ K 10
♣ A J 9 2

Rule of Extra Chances, Version 2: *when missing a queen in one suit and a king in another, and needing to take the right finesse, play the ace-king of the queen suit, and if the queen does not appear, take the finesse in the king suit.*

In the previous examples, *both* opposing hands were danger hands. If you lost a finesse to either opponent, you were about to be gobbled up in their established suit. However, there is another hand type that offers a choice of finesses, one that goes into the danger hand, the other into the non-danger hand. Guess which one you should take.

North
♠ A Q 3 2
♡ A Q 9 7
◇ 8 6
♣ K 7 5

West
♠ J 6
♡ 10 6 5
◇ K J 7 4 2
♣ Q 10 9

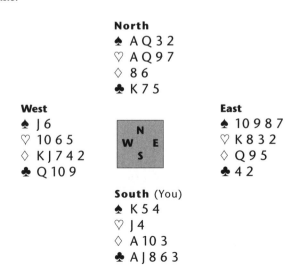

East
♠ 10 9 8 7
♡ K 8 3 2
◇ Q 9 5
♣ 4 2

South (You)
♠ K 5 4
♡ J 4
◇ A 10 3
♣ A J 8 6 3

NORTH-SOUTH VUL. DEALER SOUTH

West	North	East	South
			1♣
pass	1♡	pass	1NT
pass	3NT	all pass	

Let's look at all four hands this time. You wind up in 3NT, and West leads the ◇4. You hold off and win the third diamond, discarding a club from dummy. At this point you are pretty sure that West started with five diamonds and East, three. You have seven top tricks: three spades, two clubs, one diamond and one heart. There are several chances to develop extra tricks, but you must be careful not to allow West, the danger hand, to get the lead; take all finesses into East!

At Trick 4, run the ♡J, if it isn't covered, into East's hand. Assuming it loses, East does best to return a spade. You have already established an extra trick in hearts, the queen, and if the ♡10 drops under the ace or queen, dummy's ♡9 is your ninth trick. If that doesn't happen, well, spades have been known to divide 3-3 once every decade or so. Finally, if neither spades nor hearts are friendly, there is always the dreaded club finesse to fall back on.

With two finesses available, one heading into the danger hand, the other into the non-danger hand, guess which one you should take?

The ruffing finesse

You definitely want to be acquainted with this finesse; it can bail you out of many a touchy contract. It's most easily explained with an example:

NEITHER VUL.		DEALER SOUTH	
West	**North**	**East**	**South**
			2♠
pass	4♠	all pass	

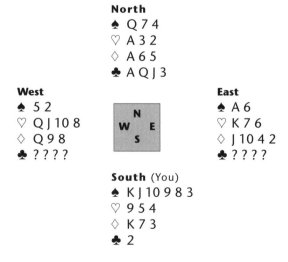

North
♠ Q 7 4
♡ A 3 2
◇ A 6 5
♣ A Q J 3

West
♠ 5 2
♡ Q J 10 8
◇ Q 9 8
♣ ? ? ? ?

East
♠ A 6
♡ K 7 6
◇ J 10 4 2
♣ ? ? ? ?

South (You)
♠ K J 10 9 8 3
♡ 9 5 4
◇ K 7 3
♣ 2

After you open a weak 2♠ bid, you wind up in 4♠, and West leads the ♡Q.

What do you count? You count nine tricks: five spades, one heart, two diamonds and one club. You also count four losers: one spade, two hearts and one diamond. A wise man once said that you should count your winners and then count your losers and if the total doesn't come to thirteen, you should count your cards!

If you win the ♡A and lead a spade, the opponents will take the ♠A, two heart tricks, and you will be faced with a possible diamond loser. True, if you *know* who has the ♣K, you can get rid of your diamond loser. If you think West has it, lead a low club to the queen; if you think East has it, play the ace and then run the queen through East, a **ruffing finesse**. No matter what East does, you will be able to get rid of your diamond loser without losing a trick. Yes, I know, this is not the ideal way to play the hand because you have basically been reduced to guessing who has the ♣K.

However, if you employ a ruffing finesse at once, it won't matter who has the ♣K! Say you win the ♡A, cash the ♣A, and lead the ♣Q, discarding a heart (if the ♣Q is not covered). Let's say it loses: the defenders can cash *one* heart, but eventually you can pitch your diamond loser on the ♣J. Notice that it did not matter who had the ♣K.

The beauty of a ruffing finesse is that it allows you to get rid of an immediate loser (the heart) and later an eventual loser, the diamond, even when the finesse loses. Finessing clubs in the normal way, by leading low to the queen, could result in immediate defeat. If the finesse loses, the opponents can take two hearts, a club, and a spade.

How does one recognize a ruffing finesse? What are the characteristics?

1. Immediate and eventual losers.
2. A singleton (or void) facing the first, third and fourth highest-ranking cards in the suit. An example: x facing AQJ(x).
3. A singleton (or void) facing the first, second, fourth and fifth highest-ranking cards in the suit. An example: x facing AKJ10(x).

4. A side-suit entry to the suit you are working with. Ruffing finesses are safer than simple finesses, *but* you must have a return entry to the suit you are establishing.

In the previous hand your club suit had the first, third and fourth ranking clubs facing a singleton. Here is a hand that features a singleton club facing the first, second, fourth and fifth ranking clubs — the tipoff.

BOTH VUL.		DEALER EAST	
West	**North**	**East**	**South**
		pass	1♠
pass	2NT[1]	pass	4NT[2]
pass	5♡[3]	pass	5NT[4]
pass	6♣[5]	pass	6♠
all pass			

1. Jacoby.
2. RKB.
3. Two keycards.
4. Confirming all keycards present.
5. King of clubs.

North
♠ A 8 3 2
♡ 8 7 5
♢ 9 7
♣ A K J 10

South (You)
♠ K Q J 10 7 6 5
♡ A 9 2
♢ A 10
♣ 3

You wind up in 6♠ and West leads the ♡K. You have eleven top tricks and somehow need to work with those clubs for your twelfth. There are two ways to play clubs for three tricks: you can lead low to the jack or play the ace-king and run the jack.

Given the precariousness of the heart position, the ruffing finesse is safer because it allows you to get rid of both hearts with zero risk. Win the ♡A, play the ♠KQ, cash the ♣AK, discarding a heart, and then lead the ♣J, discarding your other heart if the jack is not covered. Even if the ruffing finesse loses, you can dispose of your losing ♢10 on the ♣10. If the jack is covered, ruff and use the ♣10 to get rid of a red suit loser.

Did you finesse clubs the 'normal' way? You didn't think I was going to let that work for you, did you? Here's the full layout:

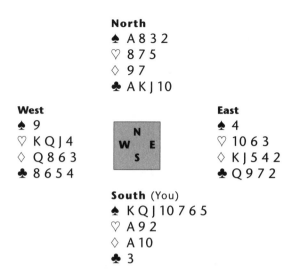

North
♠ A 8 3 2
♡ 8 7 5
♢ 9 7
♣ A K J 10

West
♠ 9
♡ K Q J 4
♢ Q 8 6 3
♣ 8 6 5 4

East
♠ 4
♡ 10 6 3
♢ K J 5 4 2
♣ Q 9 7 2

South (You)
♠ K Q J 10 7 6 5
♡ A 9 2
♢ A 10
♣ 3

Ruffing finesses may be available when a suit has already been played one or twice. To repeat: what you should be looking for are two equals facing a void, the opponents having one higher card.

The free finesse

Everybody likes a freebie once in a while. Why not? Well, when a defender leads a suit in which you are void in your hand, but facing some honor strength in the dummy, you may have just been presented with a free finesse. Look at this deal:

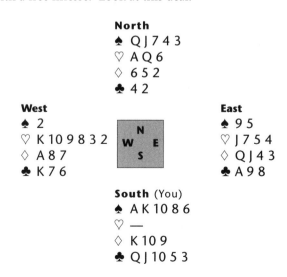

North
♠ Q J 7 4 3
♡ A Q 6
♢ 6 5 2
♣ 4 2

West
♠ 2
♡ K 10 9 8 3 2
♢ A 8 7
♣ K 7 6

East
♠ 9 5
♡ J 7 5 4
♢ Q J 4 3
♣ A 9 8

South (You)
♠ A K 10 8 6
♡ —
♢ K 10 9
♣ Q J 10 5 3

NEITHER VUL.   DEALER SOUTH

West	North	East	South
			1♠
2♡	3♠[1]	4♡	4♠
all pass			

1.   Limit raise

Opening lead: ♡10

You have just been presented with a freebie. It doesn't cost anything to insert the ♡Q. If it is covered, you ruff and life goes on; probably you will need the ◇A to be with East to make the hand. But if the ♡Q wins, you can discard two diamonds on hearts and wind up losing only one diamond and two clubs no matter who has what.

Here's a free finesse in a slam contract:

NORTH-SOUTH VUL. DEALER WEST

West	North	East	South
pass	1◇	pass	2♠
pass	3♠	pass	4◇
pass	4♠	pass	6♠
all pass			

Opening lead: ♡3

North
♠ A J 6 4
♡ K Q 10
◇ 7 6 3 2
♣ K 6

South (You)
♠ K Q 10 9 8 7
♡ —
◇ A J 9 8
♣ A Q 10

After partner opens 1◇ on a very robust suit, you restrain yourself and subside in "only" 6♠, fearing you might have missed a grand. Not to worry, partner never has the right hand. I remember Bob Hamman telling me after I had overbid (again), "Edwin, I never have the hand you want me to have, so just forget about it!" In any case, the opening lead is the ♡3. What is your plan?

Since it is highly unlikely that West would be underleading an ace against a slam contract, you should stick in the ♡10. If West was underleading the ♡J, East will play the ace, you will ruff and eventually discard two diamonds on the king and queen of hearts. If you put up the queen, and ruff out East's ace, you'll only get one diamond discard, which doesn't help; nor will a diamond discard from dummy on a club do you any good.

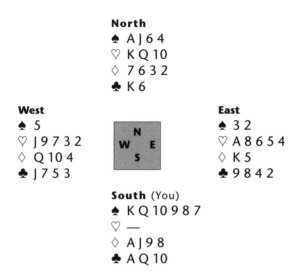

North
♠ A J 6 4
♡ K Q 10
◇ 7 6 3 2
♣ K 6

West
♠ 5
♡ J 9 7 3 2
◇ Q 10 4
♣ J 7 5 3

East
♠ 3 2
♡ A 8 6 5 4
◇ K 5
♣ 9 8 4 2

South (You)
♠ K Q 10 9 8 7
♡ —
◇ A J 9 8
♣ A Q 10

If your ♡10 fetches the ♡J from East, not the ♡A, then you just have to brace yourself to tackle diamonds.

When the opponents lead a suit in which you are void facing honor strength in the dummy, finesse options may be available; if you are missing the ace, assume your right hand opponent has it and play accordingly.

The backward finesse

Sometimes you will know, based on the bidding, that a finesse is not going to work. When this happens, you may have to play a card combination abnormally — at times, even backwards.

Although the following is not an example of playing a suit backwards, it gives you the idea.

North
♠ 10 9 7 6

South (You)
♠ A Q J 5 4

Say the bidding has told you that East cannot possibly have the ♠K; the only hope is to plunk down the ace and hope to pick off the stiff king with West. However, when you are missing a queen or a jack, and you *know* that finessing for the honors won't work, you have to try something else.

North
♠ A J 6

South (You)
♠ K 4 3

Say you know East has the ♠Q. Your only legitimate chance for three spade tricks is to play the ace-king and hope the queen drops. Again, this is not an example of a backward finesse. Patience – we'll get to it! A backward finesse when missing a queen requires strong intermediate spot cards. Among the best-known positions is this:

North
♠ A J 9

West
♠ 10 8 6 2

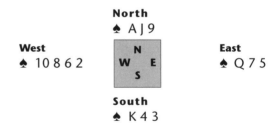

East
♠ Q 7 5

South
♠ K 4 3

Say you *know* East has the ♠Q, but this time you suspect that East has at least three spades and that playing the ♠AK will not drop the ♠Q. To compensate for this misfortune, you have been blessed with the ♠9 in the hand with the ♠J (important). You now have the wherewithal, finally, to attempt a **backward finesse**. Instead of leading low to the jack, lead the jack.

If East plays low, so do you — end of story. However, if East covers, you win the king and lead low to the nine. Yes, you must find the ♠10 with West, but given the conditions, that is your only chance. And why does the nine have to be in the same hand as the jack? Well, let's take a look at a diagram when it isn't.

North
♠ A J 3

West
♠ 10 8 6 2

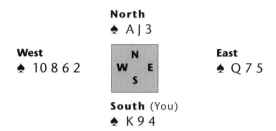

East
♠ Q 7 5

South (You)
♠ K 9 4

Say you lead the jack, queen, king. Now leading the nine doesn't help. West covers with the ten and you wind up with your same two tricks. Does this mean you cannot take a backward finesse with this combination if the nine is not with the jack? No, but if the nine is facing the jack, possession of the eight becomes necessary — in either hand.

North
♠ A J 3

West
♠ 10 6 4 2

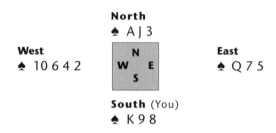

East
♠ Q 7 5

South (You)
♠ K 9 8

Now you're back in business. Lead the jack, take the queen with the king, and then run the nine. This time if West covers with the ten, you take the ace, and your eight is high. It works the same if dummy has AJ8 and you have K93.

And how about this 'backward finesse spin-off'?

North
♠ K 9 3
♡ J 9 4 2
♢ J 10 6
♣ K 9 5

```
  N
W   E
  S
```

South (You)
♠ A J 2
♡ K Q 10 7 6
♢ 8 5
♣ A Q 7

VUL. EAST-WEST		DEALER WEST	
West	**North**	**East**	**South**
1♠	pass	pass	dbl
pass	1NT	pass	2♡
pass	3♡	pass	4♡
all pass			

Opening lead: ◊K

West continues with the ◇Q and a diamond to East's ace which you ruff. You play a low heart and West wins and exits with another heart, East following. You have lost three tricks and have to avoid the loss of a spade trick. What should you do?

West needs the ♠Q to have the point count to justify an opening bid. Also, East, a player who couldn't keep the bidding open over his partner's 1♠, has already turned up with the ◇A. With this spade layout, and the ♠9 *not* in the hand with the jack and no ♠8 anywhere in sight, backward finesse possibilities look bleak. However, if East has ♠10x or a singleton ♠10 (not a bad shot since you know West has at least five spades), you can get by with ♠K9x and no ♠8. You can either start with the ace and then lead the jack, trying to pin the ten, or start with the jack, and when it is covered, win, and then lead a low spade from dummy. When East's ten appears, you win the ace, and dummy's nine is high.

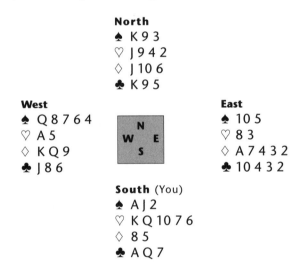

North
♠ K 9 3
♡ J 9 4 2
◇ J 10 6
♣ K 9 5

West
♠ Q 8 7 6 4
♡ A 5
◇ K Q 9
♣ J 8 6

East
♠ 10 5
♡ 8 3
◇ A 7 4 3 2
♣ 10 4 3 2

South (You)
♠ A J 2
♡ K Q 10 7 6
◇ 8 5
♣ A Q 7

Again, to pull off one of these backward finesses, which actually means taking two finesses, you have to be pretty sure you know that the normal finesse won't work.

And finally, here's an example of a backward finesse to nail a jack!

North
♠ K 6 3

West
♠ A J 4 2

East
♠ 9 7 5

South (You)
♠ Q 10 8

Say your goal in life is to take two spade tricks. With no advance information, the normal play is low to the king and, regardless of whether the king wins or loses, low to the ten next. This 'normal' play wins anytime East has the ♠J or West has ♠AJ doubleton.

But let's say you not only know from the bidding that the suit is divided 4-3, but you also *know* West has both missing honors. (You must be a pretty good player to know all of this.) Rejoice — this time you have the ♠8 in the same hand with the ♠10, which is like having the nine in the same hand with the jack: KJ(9) facing Axx or AJ(9) facing Kxx. A backward finesse is calling you. Can you hear the call?

Start with the ♠10. If West plays low, let the ten ride and take two easy tricks. But what if West covers with the jack? No problem. Win the king and lead low to the ♠8, the biggest card in your hand. If East has the ♠9, you still get two spade tricks. Remember, you made this fancy play because you *knew* where the missing spade honors were.

You have come a long way when you've learned to appreciate the value of the intermediate cards and how much easier it is to take tricks when they are attached to honors in the same hand. *AMEN.*

The Chinese finesse

In bridge language, there is a name for everything. A **Chinese finesse** is not a real finesse, it's a swindle finesse, major league style. It doesn't come up very often, but when it does, and it works, your opponent feel likes an idiot. For that reason alone it pays to be familiar with the play.

| EAST-WEST VUL. | | DEALER EAST | |
West	North	East	South
		pass	1♠
pass	2NT[1]	pass	4NT
pass	5♡	pass	5NT
pass	6♡	pass	7♠[2]
all pass			

1. Game raise in spades.
2. Flyer, big flyer.

North
♠ A J 4 3
♡ A 2
♢ K 5 3
♣ K 7 4 2

South (You)
♠ K Q 10 9 8
♡ Q 6 3
♢ A
♣ A Q J 10

You and your partner arrive at a contract of 7♠ and West leads the ♢J, East signaling encouragement. Next time you guys will play your 4-4 rather than your 5-4 fit — 7♣ is virtually cold even with a 4-1 club division. All you would have to do is ruff a diamond in the closed hand for your thirteenth trick. But that's all water over the dam. You have arrived at an impossible grand — or is it? Probably, but you should give it a shot, the old Chinese finesse shot.

Win the opening lead and lead a confident ♡Q! This is the kind of play you teach beginners never to make. You are supposed to have the jack when you lead a queen. Not this time, baby. What you have to do is hope that West, holding something like ♡Kxx(x)(x) will deem it unwise to cover. West usually assumes you have the jack to back up the queen and may even have the QJ10. If West talks himself out of covering, you have just stolen a grand.

Before you smirk at West's duck, say your hand was

♠ K Q x x x   ♡ Q J 10   ♢ A x x   ♣ A x

Now if West covers the ♡Q you have just been presented with a grand that was unmakable without help. You can use your bonus third heart winner to discard a diamond loser from dummy.

Vive le Chinese Finesse!
When all else is beyond salvation, there is always the Chinese finesse to fall back upon. However, if you use the gimmick more than once a year, you are probably overusing it.

Restricted choice

Don't get scared. This is just going to be an introduction to the topic with a simple explanation of a play that will gain you oodles of tricks over the years.

Here is an example of 'restricted choice' in action.

North
♠ K 10 4 3

West

East

South (You)
♠ A 7 6 5 2

Say you want to take five tricks in this suit. You begin correctly by leading the ace. West follows small, but East plays the quack. The what? Okay, East plays the jack or the queen — they are both the same, aren't they?

You continue and West plays the ♠9. At this point there is one card left and it is the other honor. If East has it, you should play the king; if West has it, you should play the ten. We've all been down this road before, but now you have Restricted Choice Rule 1 to see you through.

Restricted Choice Rule 1: **When the opponents hold two equally important cards, in this case the jack and the queen, and one has appeared on a previous trick, then with two cards remaining, take the finesse.**

If you trust the rule, you will insert the ♠10 in our example layout. Don't expect miracles, but if you bother to keep track, it figures to work nearly two out of three times. So do it!

How about this situation?

The mathematics of Restricted Choice gets into probability theory, but basically depends on the assumption that if East had both the queen and jack, he might have played either one; thus when he plays one honor, he is less likely to hold the other. Don't worry about the math – just play the 2:1 odds and use the rule!

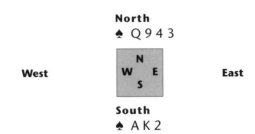

North
♠ Q 9 4 3

West

East

South
♠ A K 2

You are looking for four tricks and you do not have a count on the suit. You begin with the king and ace. On the second round East plays the ♠10. When you lead your ♠2, the opponents have two spades and West follows low. If East has the jack, you should play the queen; if West has the guarded jack, you should stick in the nine. What to do?

Does Rule #1 apply? Well, did the opponents start with two equal important cards that can influence finesse possibilities? Yes, the ten and the jack. Did one appear? Yes, the ten. Are two cards left before you played the suit at the critical juncture? Yes. So what are you waiting for? Finesse! You are now ready for Rule #2, the last restricted choice rule you have to deal with.

First, a diagram:

North
♠ Q 10 4 3

West

East

South (You)
♠ A K 2

Again you are looking for four tricks and this diagram looks a lot like the last one, but it isn't. Say you begin with the king-ace and both follow low, meaning there are two cards remaining. When you lead your ♠2, West plays low and the jack is the only card left. If East has it, you should play the queen; if West has it, you should finesse the ten. What to do? Not to worry, Restricted Choice Rule #2 is coming right up to bail you out.

Restricted Choice Rule 2: When you attack a suit that is missing one important card (here, the jack) and two cards remain outstanding in the suit, play the suit to be divided 1-1; do not finesse.

In other words, play the queen. So there you have it. The key is:
when two cards remain and the opponents started with two important cards (equals) and one has appeared, finesse. But if they started with only one important card, and two cards remain, don't
finesse — play for the drop.

Let's see how one of the rules can be applied in a full deal:

North
♠ 7 4 3
♡ A K 6
◇ K 8 4 2
♣ K 4 3

South (You)
♠ A J 10 8 5 2
♡ 7 4
◇ A 3
♣ A Q 7

You wind up in 6♠ and West leads the ♡Q to dummy's king. You
begin by leading a low spade to the jack, the right way to attack this
card combination, and West wins the queen. West exits with a
heart to dummy's ace. When you lead a second spade, East plays
low. Do you play the ace, or do you finesse the ten?

Finesse. The opponents started with two important equal cards, the
queen and the king. One has appeared and there are two cards left,
so finesse.

The full deal is at the top of the next page.

For a more complete look at Restricted Choice, refer to the *Official Encyclopedia of Bridge*.

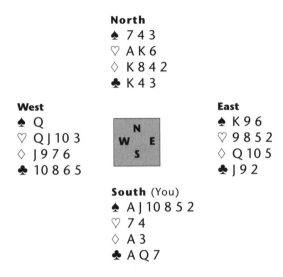

North
♠ 7 4 3
♡ A K 6
♢ K 8 4 2
♣ K 4 3

West
♠ Q
♡ Q J 10 3
♢ J 9 7 6
♣ 10 8 6 5

East
♠ K 9 6
♡ 9 8 5 2
♢ Q 10 5
♣ J 9 2

South (You)
♠ A J 10 8 5 2
♡ 7 4
♢ A 3
♣ A Q 7

The obligatory finesse

In refined circles this finesse is known as the *finesse obligata*. But what does it really mean? In plain English, it means playing low from both hands hoping something good happens.

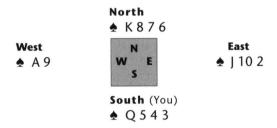

North
♠ K 8 7 6

West
♠ A 9

East
♠ J 10 2

South (You)
♠ Q 5 4 3

Let's suppose this is your trump suit in a slam contract. Are you thrilled? You each thought the other had the jack of spades. Oh, well.

It's not hopeless, however. If someone has Ax, and you have a hunch who that someone is, it can be done. Start by assuming that certain 'someone' is West, as in the diagram. (Sometimes the bidding tells you which opponent 'someone' is.) If you lead low from your hand, West does best to play low and your king will win. When you lead the suit a second time and East plays the ten or the jack, restrain yourself and play low. You know West has the ace

(East would have taken the king), so your only hope is to play West for Ax and duck. As it happens, you lose only one spade trick. A *finesse obligata*. In other words, you were 'obliged' to play low the second time — because it couldn't help to play the queen.

If you think East has the ♠A, then you must play East to have Ax.

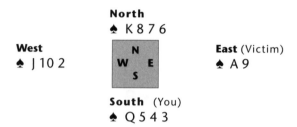

North
♠ K 8 7 6

West
♠ J 10 2

East (Victim)
♠ A 9

South (You)
♠ Q 5 4 3

This time, cross to dummy in an off suit and lead a low spade through East. East does best to play low and your queen wins. Now when you lead a second spade, you play low from dummy (you know East has the ace) and hope East has Ax. You're traveling in the fast lane now.

Here are two more examples of a *finesse obligata*.

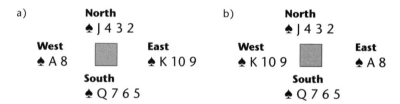

a)

North
♠ J 4 3 2

West
♠ A 8

East
♠ K 10 9

South
♠ Q 7 6 5

b)

North
♠ J 4 3 2

West
♠ K 10 9

East
♠ A 8

South
♠ Q 7 6 5

Once again this is your trump suit — a bit shaky, isn't it? Your goal is to lose only two trump tricks and for purposes of mental health you assume the suit divides 3-2. Furthermore, you can tell from the bidding that the honors are divided. How should you start? As in the previous diagrams, you have to decide who has the doubleton honor (your designated victim) and make sure that hand plays second to the first lead of a low card in the suit.

Say you pick West for your victim hoping for position (a). Start with a low card from your hand. Say West plays low and dummy's jack fetches East's king. The next time, lead low from dummy and play low from your hand. If you can't get to dummy, just lead a low card out of your hand. As it happens, West's ace pops up, so you only lose two tricks.

Now let's say you have reason to believe that East is short in spades, as in (b) on the previous page. Enter dummy with a side suit and lead a low spade to the queen and king. Next time lead a low spade and play low from dummy. East's ace appears, perforce, and you lose but two spades tricks.

Now, here's your chance to experience your own *obligata* moment:

NORTH-SOUTH VUL.		DEALER WEST	
West	**North**	**East**	**South**
1♡	dbl	2♡	2♠
pass	4♠	all pass	

Opening lead: ♡K

North
♠ K 8 6 5
♡ 9 7
♢ A K 10
♣ A Q 9 7

South (You)
♠ Q 7 3 2
♡ 5 3 2
♢ 8 4 2
♣ K J 10

West continues with the ace of hearts and a third heart which you trump in dummy, East playing the six, jack, and queen on these tricks. What now?

You have to hold your spade losers to one, and it appears that West has the ♠A to justify the opening bid. Cross to your hand with a club and lead a low spade — if West has a doubleton ace, you make the hand. If West plays low, win the king, and then strut your stuff by leading a low spade and playing low from your hand.

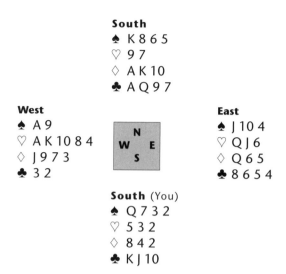

When a particular honor is marked in a certain hand, it may be necessary to assume that the honor is singleton or doubleton in order to take the maximum number of tricks.

The psychology of leading honor cards

A little secret. Even experienced defenders are not always thrilled when an honor card is led by declarer. The reality is that they can look like an idiot if they cover and they can also look like an idiot if they don't. It's not cut and dried. Here's a 'for example':

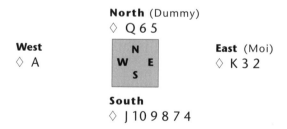

Sitting East playing with Alan Sontag, and not knowing about declarer's diamond length (I should have), I covered the queen when it was led from dummy. As you can see, this did not turn out to be a rousing success. Years have gone by and I still feel like an idiot. Nevertheless the point is clear. Whenever the declarer can afford to lead an honor card from either hand, chances of getting a cover are quite high. However, the operative word is 'afford'. You need the spots.

Therefore it pays to lead the jack in this position:

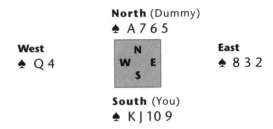

North (Dummy)
♠ A 7 6 5

West
♠ Q 4

East
♠ 8 3 2

South (You)
♠ K J 10 9

Many West players will cover thinking that because their queen is doubleton, it is worthless. They don't realize that if they play low, you may have been intending to play the ace all along and finesse the other way. In any case, your chance of seeing the queen when you play the jack is far greater than if you lead the nine or ten.

In a similar vein:

North (Dummy)
◇ A 6 3 2

West
◇ J 7

East
◇ Q 5 4

South (You)
◇ K 10 9 8

If you start with the ten, an erring West might decide to play the jack, allowing you to pick up the entire suit by winning the ace and finessing the nine on the way back.

A wonderful time to tempt a cover is with hidden length (even good players fall for this).

North (Dummy)
♣ J 4 3

West
♣ 7

East
♣ Q 9 5

South (You)
♣ A K 10 8 6 2

Leading the jack from dummy early in the play, even though you have no intention of finessing, might induce a cover.

This one could put a shaky marriage over the edge:

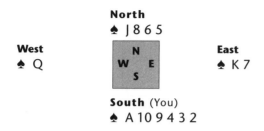

Try leading the jack from dummy and see what happens.

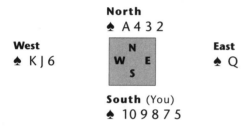

Here, why not start with the ten? If West covers, the post-mortem should be interesting.

Is it ever wrong to lead an honor when you have three honors facing one honor? Yes, even three honors might not be enough, as here:

Say your intention is to lead the jack and, if West doesn't cover, play the ace and then finesse through East. It's a noble intention, but you can't afford to waste the jack and the ace on the same trick if either opponent has four hearts. Your flamboyance will cost you a trick (assume West plays low, so you win the ace — now West has two heart winners). If you want to finesse West for the queen, lead the king and then run the jack; if you want to finesse East for the queen, lead low to the ace and then low to the jack.

It is also wrong to lead your higher or highest honor when you *don't* want the honor covered.

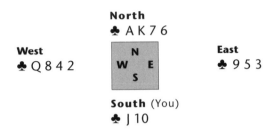

North
♣ A K 7 6

West
♣ Q 8 4 2

East
♣ 9 5 3

South (You)
♣ J 10

Say you need three club tricks, but there are no side entries to dummy. If you lead the jack, West is likely to cover and block the suit. However, if you lead the ten, West is likely to duck, hoping partner has the jack. Once West ducks and you duck, you have three club tricks.

One way of getting an opponent to duck the ace of trumps when you fear a ruff is to 'fake a finesse':

North
♡ K 8 5

West
♡ A 7

East
♡ 6 4

South (You)
♡ Q J 10 9 3 2

If you fear a side-suit ruff, begin by leading the ♡J. West may think you are about to finesse and play low. Goodbye ruffs.

When you want an opponent to cover, lead your higher or highest equal honor; when you don't want a cover, lead your second highest equal honor.

Still the best method I've ever heard of for locating a queen was told to me by my friend Patti who learned it from a friend, Alex. Patti and Alex bid to 7♠ (BKB — before Keycard Blackwood) on these cards:

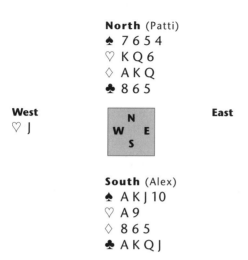

North (Patti)
♠ 7 6 5 4
♡ K Q 6
◇ A K Q
♣ 8 6 5

West
♡ J

East

South (Alex)
♠ A K J 10
♡ A 9
◇ 8 6 5
♣ A K Q J

Alex got a heart lead which he won in his hand. At Trick 2 he laid down the ♠A, both playing low, then in a heartbeat he played the king of clubs! The ♣K coming directly after the ♠A looks for all the world like the ♠K. In fact, it looked so much like the ♠K to West that he detached the ♠Q and almost had it face up on the table when in horror he saw what he had done. He frantically took back his spade and played a club, but it was much too late. Alex had no trouble picking off that doubleton queen to make his grand.

This play impressed Patti no end. She was determined to make the same play even if she had to wait years. And years it was. About three years later she wound up in a similar grand on this layout:

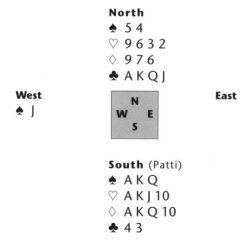

North
♠ 5 4
♡ 9 6 3 2
◇ 9 7 6
♣ A K Q J

West
♠ J

East

South (Patti)
♠ A K Q
♡ A K J 10
◇ A K Q 10
♣ 4 3

Still not playing Key Card Blackwood, Patti and her partner wound up in 7♡ and the ♠J was led. To say Patti was waiting for this moment would be an understatement. She was only sorry Alex wasn't here to watch (she had already tucked the ◊K in back of the ♡A). Like a dream she played the ♡A at Trick 2 and in perfect timing (oh, would Alex have been proud) continued with the ◊K. Even to Patti it almost looked like she was playing the king of hearts. Just as it had happened three years ago, West put a heart on the king of diamonds.

Patti said: 'Oh, I'm sorry, but I'm leading a diamond.'

'Yes, I know,' said West, 'I don't have any.'

Play Keycard Blackwood!

Beware lookalikes

Do you know the difference in the play between these two lookalikes?

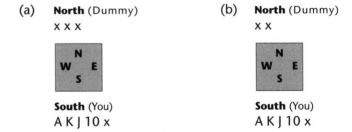

In each case you are shooting for five tricks and have plenty of dummy entries. The question is: Should you cash one high honor first in case your LHO (West) has a singleton queen, or should you finesse immediately?

The crux is whether dummy has two or three small cards. In (a), if you cash one high honor, dummy is left with *two* small cards. In (b) if you cash one high honor, dummy is left with only one small card. Does it matter? *Yes!* Study this diagram:

a)

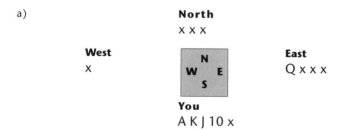

North

x x x

West

x

East

Q x x x

You

A K J 10 x

Say you cash one high honor, enter dummy, take the finesse — and West shows out. No sweat. Return to dummy, repeat the finesse, and take all five tricks. Notice that you needed, and were able, to take *two* finesses.

b)

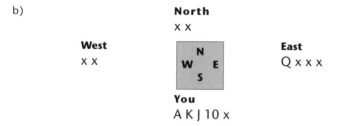

North

x x

West

x x

East

Q x x x

You

A K J 10 x

Let's try it again. You lead the ace and enter dummy to take a finesse. It works, but there are no more cards in dummy to allow you to repeat the finesse. You have to lay down the king and hope the queen falls. No luck. When East has Qxxx, East winds up with a trick. However, had you started by entering dummy and finessing immediately, you could return to dummy to repeat the finesse. You would be able to take two finesses and would not lose a trick.

With AKJ10(x) facing xxx, cash one high honor, and then finesse. With AKJ10(x)(x) facing xx, take two finesses without cashing the ace or king.

Test yourself

1.

NORTH-SOUTH VUL. DEALER SOUTH

West	North	East	South
			1◇
2♠	dbl	pass	2NT
pass	3NT	all pass	

Opening lead: ♠Q

North
♠ K 10 3
♡ A 10 9 4
◇ K 6 5 3
♣ J 2

South (You)
♠ A 6
♡ K J 7
◇ A 9 8 7
♣ 8 7 6 5

Solution on page 165

You win the ♠A at Trick 1. Now what?.

2.

BOTH VUL.   DEALER SOUTH

West	North	East	South
			2NT
pass	3NT	all pass	

Opening lead: ♠3

North
♠ 10 4
♡ 7 6 3
◇ K Q 7 5
♣ K 10 9 2

South (You)
♠ K Q 6
♡ A K 5
◇ A 4
♣ A 8 6 4 3

Solution on page 166

You try the ten from dummy but East plays the jack. Plan the play.

3.

North
♠ A 9 8
♡ J 10 4
◇ A Q J 5 4
♣ 6 5

South
♠ Q 10 7 6 5 4
♡ K Q 3 2
◇ 2
♣ A 10

NEITHER VUL.		DEALER NORTH	
West	**North**	**East**	**South**
	1◇	pass	1♠
pass	2♠	pass	4♠
all pass			

Opening lead: ♣K

Plan the play

Solution on page 167

4.

North
♠ 7 4 3
♡ A 9 8
◇ A 3 2
♣ 9 7 4 2

South (You)
♠ J 10 6
♡ Q J 10 7 6 5
◇ K J 9
♣ A

NEITHER VUL.		DEALER WEST	
West	**North**	**East**	**South**
1NT[1]	pass	pass	2♡
pass	3♡	pass	4♡
all pass			
1.	15-17 HCP.		

Opening lead: ♠A

East plays the ♠9 on the first trick. West continues with the ♠K (East playing the ♠8) and then a third spade to East's queen. East exits with the ♣Q to your ace. When you finesse in hearts, West turns up with ♡Kx. How do you continue?

Solution on page 168

5.

		DEALER SOUTH	
BOTH VUL.			
West	**North**	**East**	**South**
			1♡
pass	2◊	pass	3♡
pass	4♡	all pass	

Opening lead: ♠K

North
♠ 8 7 5
♡ 6 2
◊ A Q 6 5 2
♣ K Q 10

South (You)
♠ 9 6 2
♡ A K J 10 4 3
◊ K J
♣ A 5

West continues with the ace of spades and a third spade to East's queen. East shifts to a club.

Solution on page 169

The ball is now in your court.

6.

		DEALER WEST	
BOTH VUL.			
West	**North**	**East**	**South**
4♠	dbl	pass	5♡
pass	6♡	all pass	

Opening lead: ♠K

North
♠ 2
♡ A J 5 3
◊ A K Q J
♣ A Q 10 6

South (You)
♠ 8 4
♡ K 9 7 6 2
◊ 8 4 3
♣ K J 5

Solution on page 170

At Trick 2 West shifts to the ♣7. How do you plan to play your trump suit?

7.

North
♠ A 8 6 2
♡ K 9 3
◇ J 6 5
♣ A K 4

South (You)
♠ Q 7 3
♡ A Q J 10 8 6
◇ 9 4
♣ 9 6

BOTH VUL.		DEALER WEST	
West	**North**	**East**	**South**
1◇	dbl	pass	4♡
all pass			

Opening lead: ◇A (A from AKx)

West continues with the ◇K and a third diamond to East's queen, which you ruff. Hearts are 2-2. Plan the play.

Solution on page 171

8.

North
♠ J 6
♡ K 7 5 3
◇ K J 7
♣ J 10 9 8

South
♠ A K Q 10 9 8 7
♡ 2
◇ A 3
♣ A K 4

This is a hand where the great Giorgio Belladonna wound up declaring 6♠ after a typically complex Italian auction. West led a trump. Trumps are 2-2. Can you give yourself as many chances as Giorgio did?

Solution on page 172

9.

BOTH VUL.		DEALER SOUTH	
West	**North**	**East**	**South**
			pass
2♠[1]	dbl	pass	3◊
pass	3♠	pass	3NT
all pass			

1.   Weak.

North
♠ K
♡ A Q 10 5
◊ A Q 10 8
♣ 9 8 4 3

South
♠ Q 9 4 2
♡ K 9 4
◊ K 5 4 3
♣ 6 5

Solution on page 173

On this deal, you have a chance to win a world championship — the Venice Cup. On the next to last board of a very close final, you press to an aggressive game contract. Fortunately, West leads the ♠6, not a club, but you can't afford to give them a second chance. How will you play the hand after the ♠K wins the first trick?

Test yourself — solutions

1.

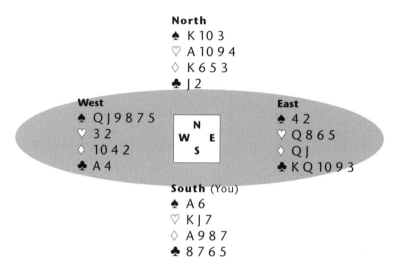

North
♠ K 10 3
♡ A 10 9 4
◇ K 6 5 3
♣ J 2

West
♠ Q J 9 8 7 5
♡ 3 2
◇ 10 4 2
♣ A 4

East
♠ 4 2
♡ Q 8 6 5
◇ Q J
♣ K Q 10 9 3

South (You)
♠ A 6
♡ K J 7
◇ A 9 8 7
♣ 8 7 6 5

NORTH-SOUTH VUL. DEALER SOUTH

West	North	East	South
			1◇
2♠	dbl	pass	2NT
pass	3NT	all pass	

Trick 1   ♠Q?

Assuming you have three spade tricks, you have eight top tricks: three spades, three hearts and two diamonds. Given the precariousness of your club stopper (?), it would not be healthy to give up the lead. The bottom line is that you have to play hearts for four tricks. What is the best play? The normal play with this heart holding is to cash the king and run the jack. However, on this hand there is bidding. West is marked with six spades and seven other cards; East has two spades and eleven other cards. It is almost twice as likely that East has any missing non-spade. Length attracts shortness; shortness attracts length. The bottom line is that you should play East for the ♡Q. After crossing to the ♠10 at Trick 2, run the ♡10. Assuming it wins, lead a heart to the jack and take the first nine tricks. Thank you very much.

BOTH VUL   DEALER SOUTH

West	North	East	South
			2NT
pass	3NT	all pass	

Trick 1   ♠3 ♠10 ♠J ?

2.

North
♠ 10 4
♥ 7 6 3
♦ K Q 7 5
♣ K 10 9 2

West
♠ A 9 7 3 2
♥ 10 4 2
♦ J 10 8 3
♣ 5

N
W E
S

East
♠ J 8 5
♥ Q J 9 8
♦ 9 6 2
♣ Q J 7

South (You)
♠ K Q 6
♥ A K 5
♦ A 4
♣ A 8 6 4 3

Win the opening lead with the ♠K (with two equals take the trick with the higher equal for deceptive purposes), and play to keep East, the hand that can hurt you by leading a spade through your queen, off lead. As you must develop at least one extra trick in clubs, the play is to lead a low club to the king and if an honor drops from West, next run the ♣10 into the West. Even if the finesse loses, you are on target to make at least one overtrick. Can anything go wrong? Yes, if East has ♣QJx and West a small singleton club, you cannot keep East off lead. You might have to try something else. Assuming West discards a heart on the second club, cash your heart and diamond winners and lead a fourth diamond from dummy, hoping West has to take the trick and lead away from the ♠A.

3.

North
♠ A 9 8
♡ J 10 4
◇ A Q J 5 4
♣ 6 5

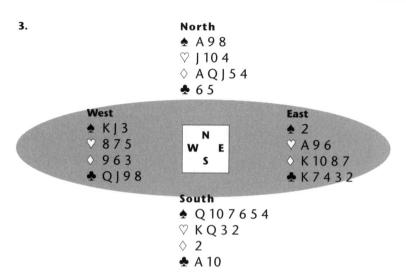

West
♠ K J 3
♡ 8 7 5
◇ 9 6 3
♣ Q J 9 8

East
♠ 2
♡ A 9 6
◇ K 10 8 7
♣ K 7 4 3 2

South
♠ Q 10 7 6 5 4
♡ K Q 3 2
◇ 2
♣ A 10

NEITHER VUL.   DEALER NORTH

West	North	East	South
	1◇	pass	1♠
pass	2♠	pass	4♠
all pass			

Trick 1   ♣Q ?

You have a club loser, a heart loser, and two possible spade losers. The first order of business is to get rid of the club loser safely. Enter the ruffing finesse. Win the ♣A, cross to the ◇A and lead the ◇Q, intending to discard a club if East plays low. If East has the ◇K as in the diagram, East has no answer. Say East covers: you ruff, cross to the ♠A, discard your losing club on the ◇J, and play a second spade. You can even afford to lose two spade tricks. The ruffing finesse, as opposed to the normal diamond finesse, is safe. Even if the ruffing finesse loses, it's a tradeoff as you have dumped a club loser. If you finesse in diamonds by leading low to the queen, you stand to lose a diamond and a club — not to mention a heart and one or two spades!

NEITHER VUL.   DEALER WEST

West	North	East	South
1NT[1]	pass	pass	2♡
pass	3♡	pass	4♡
all pass			

1.   15-17 HCP.

Trick 1   ♠A ♠3 ♠9 ♠6
Trick 2   ♠K ♠4 ♠8 ♠10
Trick 3   ♠2 ♠7 ♠Q ♠J
Trick 4   ♣Q ♣A ♣6 ♣2
Trick 5   ♡Q ♡4 ♡8 ♡2
Trick 6   ♡J ♡K ♡A ♡3

4.

North
♠ 7 4 3
♡ A 9 8
◇ A 3 2
♣ 9 7 4 2

West
♠ A K 5 2
♡ K 4
◇ Q 7 5
♣ K 6 5 3

East
♠ Q 9 8
♡ 3 2
◇ 10 8 6
♣ Q J 10 8 2

South (You)
♠ J 10 6
♡ Q J 10 7 6 5
◇ K J 9
♣ A

You have to avoid a diamond loser, but West must have the ◇Q to get up to 15 HCP. (East has already turned up with the ♠Q and a likely ♣QJ.) Furthermore, it is very unlikely that West has a doubleton diamond queen as West has already turned up with a doubleton heart — opening notrump bidders seldom have two doubletons. Given all this, it looks like a backward finesse is in your future. After drawing trumps, return to your hand and lead the ◇J. If West plays low, so do you. If West covers, win the ace, and lead a low diamond to the nine, playing East for the ◇10.

5.

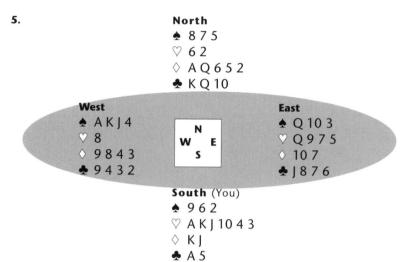

North
- ♠ 8 7 5
- ♡ 6 2
- ◇ A Q 6 5 2
- ♣ K Q 10

West
- ♠ A K J 4
- ♡ 8
- ◇ 9 8 4 3
- ♣ 9 4 3 2

East
- ♠ Q 10 3
- ♡ Q 9 7 5
- ◇ 10 7
- ♣ J 8 7 6

South (You)
- ♠ 9 6 2
- ♡ A K J 10 4 3
- ◇ K J
- ♣ A 5

BOTH VUL.		DEALER SOUTH	
West	**North**	**East**	**South**
			1♡
pass	2◇	pass	3♡
pass	4♡	all pass	

Trick 1	♠K ♠5 ♠10 ♠2
Trick 2	♠A ♠7 ♠3 ♠6
Trick 3	♠4 ♠8 ♠Q ♠9
Trick 4	♣6 ?

West continues with the ace of spades and a third spade to East's queen. East shifts to a club. This hand reduces itself to the best play in hearts for all six tricks. Since you only have two hearts in dummy, you should plan to use both for finessing purposes — in case East has ♡Qxxx, which is more likely than West having a singleton ♡Q, the reason for leading a high heart first. Win the club shift in dummy and lead a low heart to the jack. If it wins, return to dummy with a diamond and lead a low heart to the ten. If you mistakenly lead a high heart from your hand before taking a heart finesse, you lose a heart trick when East has Qxxx.

BOTH VUL.   DEALER WEST

West	North	East	South
4♠	dbl	pass	5♡
pass	6♡	all pass	

Trick 1   ♠K ♠2 ♠5 ♠4
Trick 2   ♣7 ?

6.

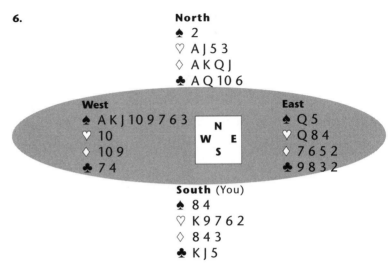

North
♠ 2
♡ A J 5 3
♢ A K Q J
♣ A Q 10 6

West
♠ A K J 10 9 7 6 3
♡ 10
♢ 10 9
♣ 7 4

East
♠ Q 5
♡ Q 8 4
♢ 7 6 5 2
♣ 9 8 3 2

South (You)
♠ 8 4
♡ K 9 7 6 2
♢ 8 4 3
♣ K J 5

Your only problem is your trump suit. With West marked with a likely eight-card spade suit and only five other cards, while East has just two spades and eleven other cards, the ♡Q figures to be with East. You would like to finesse East for the ♡Q, but unfortunately the ♡J is in dummy and neither hand has the ♡10. Still, there might be a way. Win the club lead anywhere and play the ♡A. If no ten or queen appears, you have no choice but to play the ♡K and hope the suit divides 2-2. However, if West follows with the ♡10, run the ♡J, playing East for ♡Qxx.

7.

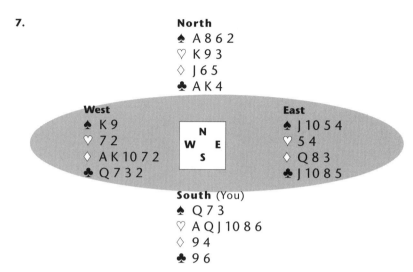

North
♠ A 8 6 2
♡ K 9 3
◇ J 6 5
♣ A K 4

West
♠ K 9
♡ 7 2
◇ A K 10 7 2
♣ Q 7 3 2

East
♠ J 10 5 4
♡ 5 4
◇ Q 8 3
♣ J 10 8 5

South (You)
♠ Q 7 3
♡ A Q J 10 8 6
◇ 9 4
♣ 9 6

BOTH VUL.   DEALER WEST

West	North	East	South
1◇	dbl	pass	4♡
all pass			

Trick 1	◇A ◇5 ◇8 ◇4
Trick 2	◇K ◇6 ◇3 ◇9
Trick 3	◇7 ◇J ◇Q ♡6
Trick 4	♡A ♡2 ♡3 ♡4
Trick 5	♡Q ♡7 ♡K ♡5

You must hold your spade losses to one trick. The normal play with this holding is to play the ace and then low to the queen. However, West needs the ♠K to justify the opening bid. Given that piece of uncomfortable information, your best hope is that West has ♠Kx. Play the ace, then a low spade towards your hand and duck, hoping the king appears.

8.

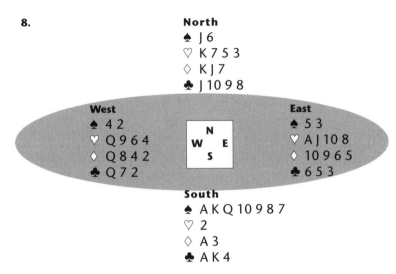

North
♠ J 6
♡ K 7 5 3
♢ K J 7
♣ J 10 9 8

West
♠ 4 2
♡ Q 9 6 4
♢ Q 8 4 2
♣ Q 7 2

East
♠ 5 3
♡ A J 10 8
♢ 10 9 6 5
♣ 6 5 3

South
♠ A K Q 10 9 8 7
♡ 2
♢ A 3
♣ A K 4

If you wish to match Giorgio's play in 6♠, you have to give yourself three chances. After drawing trumps, lead a heart to the king, chance #1. If West has the ♡A, your troubles are over, as the ♡K can be used to discard your losing club. If East has the ♡A, you next fall back on chance #2, namely playing the ♣AK, hoping the queen drops. If that doesn't happen, you are reduced to chance #3, ace of diamonds and a low diamond to the jack to get rid of the club.

9.

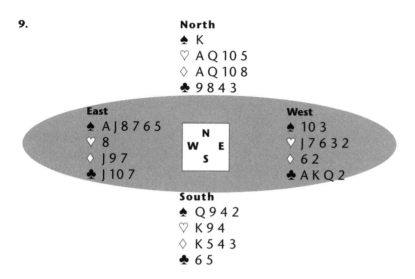

North
♠ K
♡ A Q 10 5
♦ A Q 10 8
♣ 9 8 4 3

East
♠ A J 8 7 6 5
♡ 8
♦ J 9 7
♣ J 10 7

West
♠ 10 3
♡ J 7 6 3 2
♦ 6 2
♣ A K Q 2

South
♠ Q 9 4 2
♡ K 9 4
♦ K 5 4 3
♣ 6 5

NORTH-SOUTH VUL. DEALER SOUTH

West	North	East	South
			pass
2♠	dbl	pass	3♦
pass	3♠	pass	3NT
all pass			

Trick 1   ♠6 ♠K ♠10 ♠2

German star Daniela von Arnim was declarer on this deal, which decided the 2001 Venice Cup final. After the friendly but understandable spade lead she had eight top tricks (assuming four diamond tricks), and the only hope for her contract was to bring the heart suit in for four tricks, by correctly guessing the ♡J.

After winning the opening lead with the ♠K in dummy, von Arnim played off three rounds of diamonds, East discarding a heart. At this point nine of West's cards were known — six spades and three diamonds — and East had become a strong favorite to hold heart length. Von Arnim cashed one more diamond on which East let go a club, and then bravely made the odds-on play of a heart to the nine to make her contract and give Germany the world title. Some might argue that the technically correct play was to cash only three rounds of diamonds, which would allow declarer to play the ♡A before taking the heart finesse. But that is a quibble when one considers the courage needed to count out the hand and take a first-round finesse against a jack on the next-to-last board of a world championship final.

Key ideas from Chapter 4

- When you have a two-way finesse, aim your finesse through the **danger hand** into the non-danger hand.
- If you have a one-way finesse (for a king, say), try to arrange that the opponent who can win the trick will be the non-danger hand. A **holdup play** may be one way to pull this off.
- When one opponent is known to have three (or more) cards more than his partner in one suit, play his partner for any missing jack or queen in another suit (unless the bidding tells you otherwise).
- With a choice of two finesses for queens, and not being able to safely give up the lead, cash the top cards in your longer suit to try to drop the missing honor before finessing in the shorter suit.
- When missing a queen in one suit and a king in another, cash the ace-king of the queen suit. If the queen does not drop, take the finesse against the king.
- Be alert for the possibility of a **ruffing finesse**, if you have the necessary intermediates.
- If you have the spot cards, it may be possible to take a backward finesse if you know the ordinary finesse is going to lose.
- When all else fails, you can always fall back on the **Chinese finesse**.
- Playing **Restricted Choice** gives you 2:1 odds in your favor; don't worry about why it works, just play the odds!
- Learn to recognize '**obligatory finesse**' situations.
- When you want an opponent to cover, lead your highest equal honor; when you don't want a cover, lead your second highest.

Out for the Count

*It's so simple, so very simple, that only a child
can do it.*

TOM LEHRER

This is surely one of the most important chapters in the book. Bridge is a game of counting (only to thirteen, though!) and there is no getting around it. As declarer you try to count the opponents' distribution (what this chapter is about), the opponents' high card strength (which helps you determine where the missing honors are), and the number of tricks you can take and they can take at any given moment.

Why count? The truth of the matter is that there are some hands where you can escape (luck out) without counting. However, counting gives you such a vast edge on the majority of hands that you shouldn't take the lazy way out. Count them all! This chapter will talk about some of the elements (helpers) that you can use to count a hand, from the opponents' bidding, their leads, their signals, inferences and most of all, when an opponent shows out.

WHAT YOU'RE GOING TO LEARN IN THIS CHAPTER:

- How to use the auction to get a count on the hand
- How to get a count from the opening lead and other defensive plays and signals

But first, to ease your mind, let me tell you that you only have to count one oppenent's hand, not two; you only have to count three suits, not four. Why? Because when you have the count on one hand, you have the count on the other, and when you have a count on three suits, you have a count on the fourth. All you have to do is subtract the total cards in the three suits you know from thirteen to get a count on the fourth suit. You can do it!

Counting during the bidding

Use their bidding to help you out. For example, if the bidding goes:

West	North	East	South
			(You)
1♠	pass	2♠	3♡
all pass			

Say you have a total of five spades between your hand and dummy. Credit West with five spades and East with three. Suddenly you have a count on one suit and you only need get a count on two more. To make counting even easier, simply count the hand that has the known longer suit. Here, zero in on West, the hand with the known five-card spade suit. It's like having a head start.

Preempts give you wonderful head starts.

West	North	East	South
2♡[1]	dbl	pass	2♠
all pass			

1. Weak

West figures to have six hearts and, therefore, only seven other cards. Zero in on West.

Speaking of preempts, players have been known to have one fewer card than you might suspect in the preempted suit. They are most apt to 'cheat a card' in third seat after two passes not vulnerable vs. vulnerable, or, for that matter, almost any time they are not vulnerable and you are. Players nowadays find it irresistible to preempt with one less card than expected when not vulnerable. P.S. Trust the vulnerable preempts.

It pays to know your opponents' bidding system. Do they play five-card majors in all seats, or will they open with a four-card major suit in third or fourth? Will they support a one-level major-suit response with three cards or do they require four? Will they open 1NT with a five-card major? Do they play support doubles? Assume your opponents are playing support doubles (a convention to be familiar with), and the bidding goes:

West	North	East	South
			(You)
1♣	pass	1♠	2♡
all pass			

Say a club is led and the spades in dummy are ♠643 facing ♠A108 in your hand. If the opponents are playing support doubles, West's pass over 2♡ denies three spades (a 'double' shows three spades, a raise promises four). Therefore, East has at least five spades. But if East had six spades, he probably would have rebid 2♠. Assume spades are 5-2 and count the East hand, the hand with the longer suit.

Inferential counts

Sometimes you can *infer* the count of a suit, particularly a major suit, based not only on what the opponents have bid but on what they haven't bid!

For example, say the bidding goes:

West	North	East	South
			(You)
1♢	pass	1♠	2♣
pass	3♣	all pass	

Say a spade is led and dummy has the ♡Q5 and you the ♡J107. The opponents have eight hearts, and neither one has mentioned the suit. Strange. Surely if either opponent had five hearts, the suit would have been bid; you can assume hearts are 4-4. Furthermore, once you assume hearts are 4-4, you can infer that East has at least five spades. If East had four hearts and four spades, East would have responded 1♡, not 1♠. Count the East hand; you already know nine of that player's cards!

Now consider this bidding sequence:

West	North	East	South
			(You)
1♣	pass	1♠	3◇
all pass			

Say a spade is led and East turns up with four spades. You can infer that East cannot have four hearts or else East's original response would have been 1♡.

Try this one:

West	North	East	South
			(You)
1♣	pass	1♡	pass
2♡	dbl	pass	2♠
all pass			

Dummy has three hearts and you have three hearts. How are the remaining seven hearts divided? Surely East must have four and West, three. What else could it be?

Short diamonds and short clubs — a big giveaway

When an opponent opens the bidding 1◇ and turns up with exactly three diamonds, assume an original distribution of 4-4 in the majors with a doubleton club. That is by far the most likely distribution for a short diamond opening. Can you imagine how well you can play a hand when you know opener's exact distribution early in the hand? Yes, with mirrors.

When an opponent opens 1♣ and is known to have exactly three clubs, the opener is either 4-4 in the majors with a doubleton diamond or 4-3-3-3 with one four-card major. If the 1♣ bidder turns up with a doubleton diamond, assume 4-4 in the majors. If the 1♣ bidder turns up with three hearts, assume a 4-3-3-3 pattern with four spades. If the 1♣ bidder turns up with three spades, assume a 3-4-3-3 pattern. It's almost like cheating.

Counting during the play

The opening lead

The opening lead is frequently a count card; for example, the deuce playing fourth-best leads against notrump shows a four-card suit. To proceed a little further: say West leads the ◇2 against your notrump contract and later in the play turns up with a singleton heart. This means West started with eight black cards. Presumably those eight cards are divided 4-4, for if they were divided 5-3, the presumption is that West would have led from the five-card suit.

When a defender leads partner's unsupported suit, the lead should be a count card — low from three, high from a doubleton. Say the bidding has gone like this:

West	North	East	South
			(You)
1◇	pass	1♡	2♠
all pass			

These are the hearts you see when the dummy comes down:

North
♡ A 8 7

South (You)
♡ 10 6 4

If the opening lead is the ♡9, this lead figures to be from shortness. With ♡9xx, the proper lead from three small in an unsupported suit is the lowest card. Furthermore, the lead figures to be from a doubleton, not a singleton. If it were a singleton, East would have started with ♡KQJxxx and surely would have rebid the suit. Wouldn't you?

Now suppose the opening lead is the ♡2. This could be a singleton, but the more likely possibility is that it is low from three, meaning East has exactly four hearts. Say you play low and East wins the king. That tells you that West has the ♡Qxx and East ♡KJxx (if West has the ♡QJx, the queen is the proper lead).

Finally, suppose West leads the ♡3. This could be from ♡32 double-ton or his lowest from three. You will surely be able to work it out when you see West's next heart — perhaps sooner. If it is higher than the ♡3, you know the lead was from a three-card suit; if it is the deuce, you know it's a doubleton.

Subsequent plays in the suit that has been led

If your opponent leads the ♠4 from ♠Q8742 (fourth best leads) and wishes to show that the lead was from a five-card suit, the ♠2 is played on the next round of spades, if possible. High-lows at notrump from a player who has led from length generally show a five-card suit. However, the lead of a spot card followed by the play (or discard) of two lower spot cards indicate a six-card suit. For example, if the opening leader started with ♠Q107432, the proper lead is the ♠4, followed by the ♠3 and then the ♠2 in that order (perhaps two discards in the suit were available).

Watch their signals

Frequently the opponents' attitude signals (high-lows to show a doubleton, etc.) plus their count signals can help you with the count. Remember, whenever they give each other count, you are right there to intercept the message. Every little piece of informa-tion might help! In our examples, we'll assume they are playing 'standard' count (high-low shows an even number of cards, low-high shows an odd number). If they are playing 'upside down' count signals, everything is reversed — high-low shows an odd number and low-high, an even number.

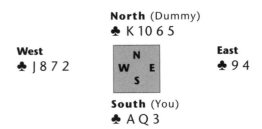

North (Dummy)
♣ K 10 6 5

West　　　　　　　　**East**
♣ J 8 7 2　　　　　　♣ 9 4

South (You)
♣ A Q 3

Facing an otherwise entryless dummy, you begin by leading the queen, hoping they each think their partner has the ace and will give each other count. How clever you are! You, on the other hand, will see how the suit is dividing. West will play the ♣8, second highest from four, and East will play the ♣9, top of a doubleton. When you continue with the ace, both opponents will play lower clubs. If they are telling the truth, each started with an even number of clubs. When you lead a third club, you can, with reasonable certainty, insert the ten. Notice that if you started by playing the ace, there would be far less reason for the opponents to give each other count.

North (Dummy)
♣ 7 6

West
♣ J 8 3

East
♣ Q 10 5 4

South (You)
♣ A K 9 2

Assume hearts are trumps and your plan is to trump clubs in dummy. Say you start with the king, a card that is more likely to elicit a count card from the defense, and continue with the ace and a low club, ruffing in dummy.

If West has played the 3-8-J (low-high showing an odd number) and East the 5-4-10 (high-low showing an even number) the inference is that West started with three clubs and East four.

Revising your count

No, not when they drop their cards face up. It is normal to assume a particular bid shows 'expected length'. Nonetheless, you must stay flexible. For example:

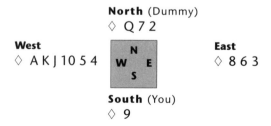

North (Dummy)
♢ Q 7 2

West
♢ A K J 10 5 4

East
♢ 8 6 3

South (You)
♢ 9

West has opened the bidding 3♢ and you expect West to have seven diamonds and East a doubleton. But then West leads a top diamond and East plays low, showing three diamonds (or just possibly ◊Kx if West has led the ace). You should revise your count and credit West with six diamonds and go from there.

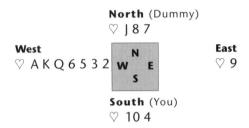

North (Dummy)
♡ J 8 7

West
♡ A K Q 6 5 3 2

East
♡ 9

South (You)
♡ 10 4

West has bid and rebid hearts and you expect West to have six hearts. But when West leads two top hearts and East discards on the second heart you must revise your estimate. West is known to hold seven hearts and surely that is the hand to count.

Showing out

As witnessed by the previous example, the single most decisive clue to getting a count in any suit is when an opponent shows out. You now have a known count on that suit and that may be a springboard for a count on the other suits. As a reminder, when someone shows out early and their partner has serious length, you know which hand to count.

Bringing it all together

Two-way suits

A **two-way suit** is a combination of cards in one suit where you have a two possible lines of play. For example with

A K 10 x

Q x x

you can take a third-round finesse or play for a 3-3 break.

Counting really pays off when you have a 'two-way' suit. This is a suit which can be played in one of two ways. It may entail a two-way finesse for a queen. For example, if you have the KJx in dummy facing A10x in your hand, you have a two-way suit, as you can finesse the queen in either direction. Two-way suits are generally saved until the bitter end for at least two good reasons: sometimes you are playing against friends or relatives who lead the suit, obviating the guess; second, if you can get a count on the suit, you will have a better chance of figuring out who has the missing honor.

When missing an important card in a two-way suit, assume the hand that started with the greater length in the suit has the missing honor card. However, if the bidding tells you that one opponent needs the missing honor to justify the bidding, play that opponent for the missing honor willy-nilly.

This brings to mind a famous Oswald Jacoby story: Once Ozzie was playing a hand and had a two-way finesse in diamonds missing the queen. He had counted the other suits and knew that his LHO had started with five diamonds and his RHO with only two. The odds were 5-2 that West, his LHO, had the ◊Q. As he was about to finesse through West, East, to his right, accidentally dropped his cards exposing the ◊Q. At that point, Jacoby said, 'I've just decided to revise my count!'

Here are some other common two-way suits that you surely are familiar with:

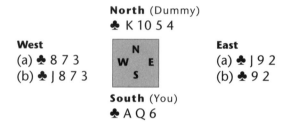

North (Dummy)
♣ K 10 5 4

West
(a) ♣ 8 7 3
(b) ♣ J 8 7 3

East
(a) ♣ J 9 2
(b) ♣ 9 2

South (You)
♣ A Q 6

Say you need four club tricks to make your contract. Begin with the queen, then the ace, and finally the ♣6 towards dummy's ♣K10. If the clubs are divided 3-3 as in (a), play the king and drop East's jack. However, if the clubs are divided 4-2 as in (b), insert the ♣10. How can you tell? Count the other suits before you touch clubs. Don't even think of playing a two-way suit early. Frequently, you will be able to get a complete count on the other suits so you will know whether it is (a) or (b).

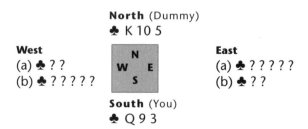

North (Dummy)
♣ K 10 5

West
(a) ♣ ? ?
(b) ♣ ? ? ? ? ?

East
(a) ♣ ? ? ? ? ?
(b) ♣ ? ?

South (You)
♣ Q 9 3

This is a suit you hope they lead. If they do, you have two sure tricks, but if they don't, you have to locate the ♣J all by your lonesome. And just how do you do that without peeking? You *count* — the other suits, that's how. Let's say that your count reveals that West started with two clubs and East five. East is more than twice as likely to hold the ♣J so play East for the jack. However, if the count tells you that West has the club length (b), then play West for the ♣J.

North (Dummy)
♣ A 9 3

West
(a) ♣ Q 7 6
(b) ♣ 7 6

East
(a) ♣ J 8 2
(b) ♣ Q J 8 2

South (You)
♣ K 10 5 4

Say you need three club tricks and you begin by leading low to the nine which loses to East's jack. Later you play the ace and then low to the K-10. If the clubs are 3-3 (a), play the king; but if clubs are 4-2 (b), finesse the ten. Guess how you can tell.

North (Dummy)
♣ A K Q 9

West
(a) ♣ 10 7 6 5
(b) ♣ 7 6 5

East
(a) ♣ J 3
(b) ♣ J 10 3

South (You)
♣ 8 4 2

Once again you need four club tricks. You begin by playing the ace-king, noticing the jack from East. What next? If the jack is an honest card (a), return to your hand and lead low to the nine. If East is teasing you and has the ten (b), cash the queen and the nine will be high. It would be nice to get these positions right, wouldn't it? You will if you count — the other suits.

Pep talk from the coach

Obviously you have plenty to think about, but the trick is to be able to put it all together without putting your opponents to sleep waiting for you to get a count. Don't panic! Counting isn't going to happen overnight, but if you aren't 'in the mode' it's time to start. To ease the pain, keep in mind you are working with small numbers. And those small numbers get smaller. Say you know someone has a six-card suit. That means they only have seven other cards. Each time the count in another suit unfolds, that number 'seven' gets smaller. Say you know someone is likely to have 5-4 distribution from the bidding. That means they only have four other cards to worry about. Piece of cake.

Start by using their bidding and their 'show outs' to help you. Those are the two biggies. As your confidence grows, so will your counting ability. Good luck — your game is about to improve dramatically!

Practice hands

NORTH-SOUTH VUL.   DEALER EAST

West	North	East	South
		pass	1◊
4♡	5◊	all pass	

Opening lead: ♡K

Hand 1

North
♠ A 7 3
♡ 4 3 2
◊ A 10 9 8 6
♣ K 2

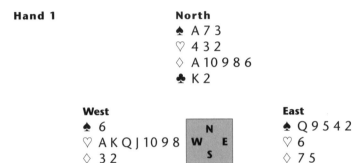

West
♠ 6
♡ A K Q J 10 9 8
◊ 3 2
♣ Q 10 9

East
♠ Q 9 5 4 2
♡ 6
◊ 7 5
♣ J 7 5 4 3

South (You)
♠ K J 10 8
♡ 7 5
◊ K Q J 4
♣ A 8 6

West begins with three rounds of hearts, East discarding a low spade and a low club. When you see East discard on the second heart, you know that West started with seven hearts and so West is the hand to count. You have a two-way suit, spades, and so the count will be important. When you draw trumps, you notice that both opponents started with two trumps. Therefore, West has started with nine known red cards. In order to complete the count, play the king and ace of clubs, and ruff a club in dummy. Even though clubs may appear to be an irrelevant suit, it is not. It will help you with the spade count!

When West follows to three rounds of clubs, you know twelve cards in the West hand: seven hearts, two diamonds and three clubs. Therefore, West has at most one spade. Now, and only now, is it safe to attack spades. Lead a spade to the ace, ridding West of his singleton, and lead a spade to the jack, secure that the jack will win the trick.

Key points
- When one defender turns up with a long suit, count that defender's hand.
- When you have a two-way side suit (as opposed to a two-way trump suit), try to play that suit last.
- If you can get a count on three suits, you have a count on the fourth.

Hand 2

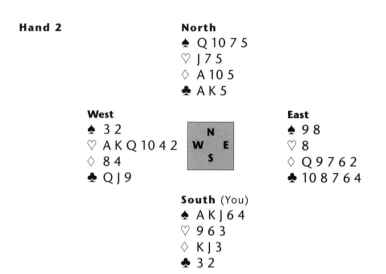

North
♠ Q 10 7 5
♡ J 7 5
◇ A 10 5
♣ A K 5

West
♠ 3 2
♡ A K Q 10 4 2
◇ 8 4
♣ Q J 9

East
♠ 9 8
♡ 8
◇ Q 9 7 6 2
♣ 10 8 7 6 4

South (You)
♠ A K J 6 4
♡ 9 6 3
◇ K J 3
♣ 3 2

BOTH SIDES VUL.   DEALER SOUTH

West	North	East	South
			1♠
2♡	3♡[1]	pass	3♠[2]
pass	4♠[3]	all pass	

1. Limit raise or better in spades.
2. Not interested in game facing a limit raise.
3. Better than a limit raise.

Opening lead: ♡K

West cashes three rounds of hearts, East discarding a club and a diamond, and shifts to the queen of clubs. The entire hand depends upon locating the diamond queen, a card which can be finessed in either direction. Time to count. (Don't be like the fellow who always finessed through the defender he disliked the most because it gave him so much more pleasure when the finesse worked.) The trick is to play the other suits first in order to get a count on the two-way suit, diamonds. Remember, you only need a count on three suits and you already have it on one, since you know West started with six hearts.

When you draw trumps, West turns up with two spades, making eight major-suit cards. Now test the clubs: play the ace and king and ruff a club. When you do, West follows to all three clubs. Let's review: West started with six hearts, two spades, and at least three clubs. (Nobody has shown out of clubs, so you can't be 100% sure of the club count.) In any case, West started with no more than two diamonds which means East started with at least five. Since East is at least 2½ times as likely as West to have the queen of diamonds, lead a diamond to the ace and a diamond to the jack, playing East for the queen.

Key point
• When missing a vital card, and that card can be finessed in either direction, do not play the player you dislike the most for the card, but rather the player who started with the greater length in the suit. In other words, you have to count. Sorry about that.

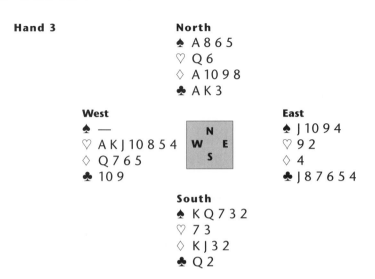

NEITHER VUL.   DEALER EAST

West	North	East	South
		pass	pass
4♡	dbl	pass	4♠
all pass			

Opening lead: ♡A

(Ace from AKx at Trick 1 only)

Hand 3

North
♠ A 8 6 5
♡ Q 6
◇ A 10 9 8
♣ A K 3

West
♠ —
♡ A K J 10 8 5 4
◇ Q 7 6 5
♣ 10 9

East
♠ J 10 9 4
♡ 9 2
◇ 4
♣ J 8 7 6 5 4

South
♠ K Q 7 3 2
♡ 7 3
◇ K J 3 2
♣ Q 2

West cashes two hearts, East playing high-low, so credit West with seven hearts. At Trick 3 West shifts to the ♣10, which you win with the queen. When you lead the spade king from your hand, West discards a heart. Ouch! The idea here is to get a count on the hand so you will know how to tackle diamonds, a two-way suit. It can't hurt to play two more high spades, leaving East with a high trump, and then two more rounds of clubs. As it happens, West discards a heart on the third club, so the count is complete.

West started with seven hearts (known from the bidding and East's signal), no spades, two clubs (West has shown out of both suits) and therefore four diamonds. If West started with four diamonds, East started with only one. Play the ◇K, removing East's singleton, and run the ◇J through West. All the defense can manage is East's high trump.

Key point
- Although it is likely that a player who is long in one suit will be quite short in another (length attracts shortness; shortness attracts length), it is not 100% certain. Counting the other suits is the surer way to go if you have the luxury of doing so.

Hand 4

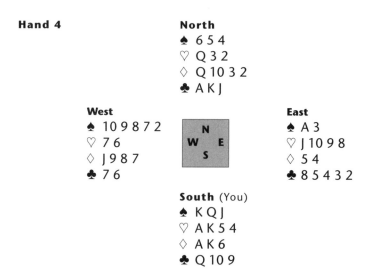

North
- ♠ 6 5 4
- ♡ Q 3 2
- ◇ Q 10 3 2
- ♣ A K J

West
- ♠ 10 9 8 7 2
- ♡ 7 6
- ◇ J 9 8 7
- ♣ 7 6

East
- ♠ A 3
- ♡ J 10 9 8
- ◇ 5 4
- ♣ 8 5 4 3 2

South (You)
- ♠ K Q J
- ♡ A K 5 4
- ◇ A K 6
- ♣ Q 10 9

NEITHER VUL.   DEALER SOUTH

West	North	East	South
			2NT
pass	6NT	all pass	

Opening Lead: ♠10

East wins the spade ace and returns the suit. You have eleven top tricks with chances for a twelfth in either red suit. Also, you have a two-way suit in diamonds, which means diamonds is the last suit you will play. When you have all the tricks but one, the proper technique is to take your winners in those suits in which you cannot possibly score an extra trick — clubs and spades — before you attack the problem suit. The reason is that you might get a friendly discard, like a diamond or a heart.

Say you cash your remaining high spade next, and East discards a club. Notice that you need not fear setting up spade winners for West because you have all the rest of the tricks but one — either you will take the last trick or they will. You now know that West started with five spades. Next cash three club tricks. If West is clever, West will discard a spade on the third club, the suit you already have a count on. So West started with five spades and two clubs. You have a count on two suits and you only need a count on one more. Your next move is to cash three rounds of hearts, hoping they will break 3-3. Dreamer — not in this chapter! In this chapter you have to count!

As it happens, West turns up with a doubleton heart. Translation: West started with five spades, two hearts, two clubs, and therefore four diamonds. The play in the two-way diamond suit is now clear. Play the ace and king and if the jack hasn't appeared, lead a diamond to the ten. Are you a counter, or what?

Key points

When you have all the tricks but one:

- Do not worry about setting up tricks for the opponents in their long suits (clubs and spades).
- Play the suits where you cannot develop any extra tricks first (clubs and spades).
- Save the two-way suit for last (diamonds).
- Count!

Test yourself

In the first few questions, you will be shown the hearts in your hand and in the dummy. Though the opponents have been in the bidding, you wind up playing the hand. When the dummy comes down your job is to determine from the bidding how their hearts are divided, even though a heart may not have been led.

North (Dummy)
♡ 9 4

West　　♡ ?　**East**　　♡ ?

South (You)
♡ Q J 6

Solutions on page 195

1. West opens 1♡ and East raises to 2♡.
2. West opens 2♡.
3. East opens 3♡ in third seat, not vulnerable.
4. East overcalls North's opening 1◇ bid with 1♡, West never bids and leads the ♡8.
5. Same scenario as (4), but West leads the ♡2.
6. The opponents have both been in the bidding, but hearts have never been mentioned.
7. West opens 1♣, partner passes, East bids 1♡, you overcall 1♠ and West makes a support double.

Now assume you are playing a notrump contract and the opponents are leading fourth-best. In addition, when they lead partner's unsupported suit (at a suit or notrump) they lead high from a doubleton and low from any three cards. Determine from the clues given how the hearts are breaking in the opponents' hands.

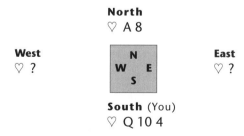

North
♡ A 8

West　　♡ ?　**East**　　♡ ?

South (You)
♡ Q 10 4

8. Hearts is an unbid suit and West leads the ♡2.
9. Hearts is an unbid suit and West leads the ♡3 and later plays the ♡2.

North
♡ A 8

West
♡ ?

East
♡ ?

South (You)
♡ Q 10 4

10. East overcalls hearts and West leads (a) the ♡2 (b) the ♡3 (c) the ♡5.

11. West leads the ♡7, you play low and East wins the ♡K. When East returns the suit you play the ♡10 and West plays the ♡J.

Now for some practice reading count signals.

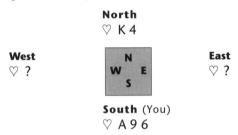

North
♡ K 4

West
♡ ?

East
♡ ?

Solutions on page 195

South (You)
♡ A 9 6

12. Spades are trumps and you plan to ruff a heart in the dummy. You lead the six to the king, come back to the ace and ruff the nine. West plays the 3-10-J and East the 2-5-7. Assuming they are giving each other standard signals, what do you make of the heart position?

13. Same situation, but this time West plays 8-2-7 and East 5-3-10. Now, what do you make of the heart position?

14. Which of the following can be classified as two-way suits, meaning there might be more than one way to attack the suit?

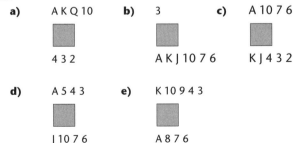

a)	A K Q 10	**b)**	3	**c)**	A 10 7 6
	4 3 2		A K J 10 7 6		K J 4 3 2

d)	A 5 4 3	**e)**	K 10 9 4 3
	J 10 7 6		A 8 7 6

15.

North
♠ 9 7 5 4
♡ A 8 4 3
♢ 9 4 3 2
♣ 4

N
W E
S

South (You)
♠ A 10
♡ 9 6 5
♢ 10 7
♣ A K Q 10 8 7

NEITHER VUL.		DEALER WEST	
West	**North**	**East**	**South**
1♢	pass	2♢	3♣
all pass			

Solution on page 196

Opening lead: the ♡K. Any early clues as to the distribution of the East-West hands?

16.

North
♠ 6 3 2
♡ 9 8 4
♢ 10 5
♣ A 10 8 7 6

N
W E
S

South (You)
♠ A 10
♡ A 6 3
♢ A Q J 9 8 4
♣ K 2

NEITHER VUL.		DEALER WEST	
West	**North**	**East**	**South**
pass	pass	3♠	3NT
pass	pass	pass	

Solution on page 196

Opening lead: ♠4. East plays the ♠J. Do you take the trick? What is your plan?

BOTH VUL.   DEALER SOUTH

West	North	East	South
			2NT
pass	7NT	all pass	

Opening lead: ♣10

17.

North
♠ A K 9
♡ K Q J
♢ K J 8 5
♣ J 5 2

South (You)
♠ Q J 8 3
♡ A 10 9
♢ A 10 9
♣ A K Q

a) How many top tricks do you have?
b) Do you have a two-way suit?
c) Which suits do you play first?
d) Say you begin with four rounds of spades, discarding a diamond from dummy. The opponents each have three spades, West discarding a club, East a heart on the fourth spade. When you continue with three rounds of hearts, all follow. Next, you cash your two remaining winning clubs, East discarding a diamond on the third club. What is the count on the hand, and whom do you play for the ◊Q?

Solution on page 197

NEITHER VUL.   DEALER EAST

West	North	East	South
		3◊	3♠
4♡	4♠	pass	pass
5◊	5♠	all pass	

Opening lead: ♡K
(King from AKx at the five-level or higher)

18.

North
♠ K Q 9 4
♡ 7 6
♢ A 3
♣ Q J 6 3 2

South (You)
♠ A J 10 7 6 5
♡ Q 8
♢ 4
♣ A 8 7 5

West cashes the ♡A next, East playing the ♡J and then the ♡10. At Trick 3 West shifts to the ◊2 to dummy's ace. When you draw trumps, you discover that East started with one spade, West two. How do you play the clubs?

Solution on page 197

Test yourself — solutions

1. West has five hearts, East three.
2. West has six hearts, East two.
3. East may have six or seven hearts (if a heart is led, the count should be clarified).
4. West has two hearts, East six.
5. West has three hearts, East five.
6. Hearts figure to be 4-4. If either player had five, the suit would have been mentioned.
7. West has three hearts, East five; a support double shows three.
8. Hearts figure to be 4-4.
9. West has five hearts, East three
10. a) When the deuce is led, assume West has three hearts.
    b) *and* (c) When the three or the five is led, watch West's next card like a hawk. If it's a lower spot, West started with a doubleton; if it is higher, play West for three hearts.
11. West must have started with J97.
12. West appears to have started with three hearts, East five (low-high shows an odd number).
13. Both players appear to have four hearts (high-low shows an even number).
14. They all are! Your count, if you can get it in time, determines how you play the suit.
    a) After you play the ace and king, you have to decide whether to play the queen or lead low to the ten.
    b) Although it is normal to play low to the jack, if your count tells you that West has a doubleton, you might as well play the ace and king, because you cannot pick up Qxxx on your right.
    c) If the count tells you that one of your opponents started with a singleton, you can finesse through the other one. If your count tells you they are 2-2, bang down the king and ace.
    d) This is a toughie. Assuming you play for split honors, lead the jack if you think West has a doubleton honor, and lead toward the jack if you think East has a doubleton honor.
    e) If the count tells you that East started with a singleton, play the ace and, if an honor falls, lead low to the ten. If it tells you that West has a singleton, lead low to the king, and if an honor drops from West, run the ten through East.

NEITHER VUL.   DEALER WEST

West	North	East	South
1◇	pass	2◇	3♣
all pass			

Trick 1   ♡K ?

15.

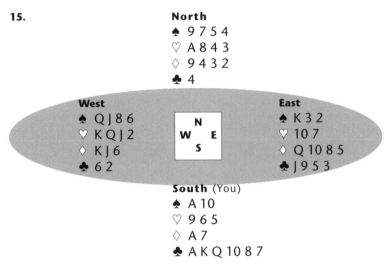

Given the bidding, East figures to have four diamonds and West, three. If so, West started with 4-4-3-2 distribution and the percentage play in clubs (given that East has four) is to lead low to the ten!

NEITHER VUL.   DEALER WEST

West	North	East	South
pass	pass	3♠	3NT
pass	pass	pass	

Trick 1   ♠4 ♠2 ♠J ?

16.

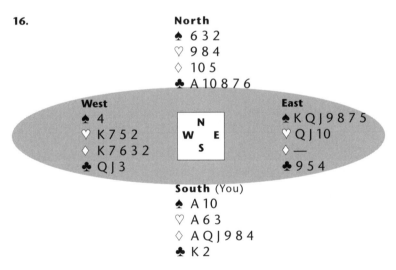

Do not hold up! The lead tells you that a singleton is being led (you can see the deuce and trey). Win the trick, cross to the ♣A, and run the ◇10. Even if it loses, West will not have a spade to return and you have nine winners. If you duck the opening lead and West switches to a heart, you could be in big trouble.

17.

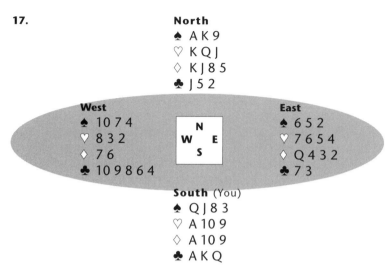

North
♠ A K 9
♡ K Q J
◇ K J 8 5
♣ J 5 2

West
♠ 10 7 4
♥ 8 3 2
◇ 7 6
♣ 10 9 8 6 4

East
♠ 6 5 2
♥ 7 6 5 4
◇ Q 4 3 2
♣ 7 3

South (You)
♠ Q J 8 3
♡ A 10 9
◇ A 10 9
♣ A K Q

BOTH VUL.		DEALER SOUTH	
West	**North**	**East**	**South**
			2NT
pass	7NT	all pass	

Trick 1   ♣10 ?

a) Twelve.

b) Yes, diamonds.

c) Everything but diamonds!

d) The hand counts out. West is known to have started with three spades, three hearts, five clubs and two diamonds. If West started with two diamonds, East started with four. That means East is twice as likely to own the ◇Q. Play East for the missing lady.

18.

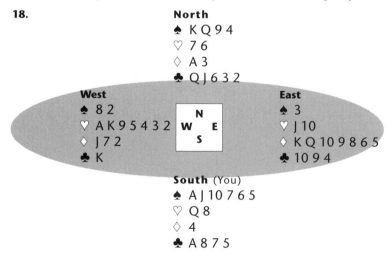

North
♠ K Q 9 4
♡ 7 6
◇ A 3
♣ Q J 6 3 2

West
♠ 8 2
♥ A K 9 5 4 3 2
◇ J 7 2
♣ K

East
♠ 3
♥ J 10
◇ K Q 10 9 8 6 5
♣ 10 9 4

South (You)
♠ A J 10 7 6 5
♡ Q 8
◇ 4
♣ A 8 7 5

NEITHER VUL.		DEALER EAST	
West	**North**	**East**	**South**
		3◇	3♠
4♡	4♠	pass	pass
5◇	5♠	all pass	

Trick 1	♡K ♡6 ♡J ♡8
Trick 2	♡A ♡7 ♡10 ♡Q
Trick 3	◇2 ◇A ◇10 ◇4
Trick 4	♠4 ♠3 ♠A ♠2
Trick 5	♠5 ♠8 ♠K ◇9

West is known to have seven hearts, at least three diamonds, two spades, and therefore at most one club. Given your lack of club spots, the only hope to make the hand is that West's singleton club is the king. Play the ace!

Key ideas from Chapter 5

- Try to make **counting** a habit.
- Use the opponents' **bidding**, **leads**, and **count signals** to help you .
- You need only count one hand — the opponent who first turns up with a long suit.
- Counting a hand means counting three suits; once you know three, you know four.
- Try to save your two-way suit until the bitter end in case you can get a count on the hand.
- When missing an important card, assume the player with the greater original length in the suit has it.
- Even if you find you are having trouble counting (join the club), don't give up. The more you do it, the easier it becomes.
- There are three kinds of bridge players — those that count and those that don't!

No Exit

How strange... the only winning move is not to play.
FROM 'WARGAMES' (MOVIE 1983)

Are you wondering what the title of this chapter means? It refers to throwing an opponent in at a time when that opponent has no safe exit cards and therefore must present you with a trick. We are talking about a **strip and endplay**, also called a **strip and throw-in play**, also called an **elimination play**.

Before you can pull off one of these 'strips', it helps to know what to look for, because not all hands fit the mold.

The first example hand (next page) illustrates the necessary conditions:

1. A trump suit that allows you to draw trumps and still leave at least one trump in each hand; 4-4 or 5-4 trump fits lend themselves to this type of play.
2. A side suit that makes you nauseated to look at (think Jxx facing Qxx) that you would much prefer the opponents to lead first. From here on in this will be called the 'off-limits' suit.
3. A second side suit that can be stripped or eliminated from both your hand and dummy either by trumping (think Ax facing Kxx) or by cashing out your tricks in a no-loser side suit (think AKx facing Qxx).
4. An *equally* divided side suit in which you have an inevitable loser or losers (think Ax facing xx, Axx facing Kxx, even xx facing xx or xxx facing xxx).

Now let's take a look at our example hand and see if you can identify these four conditions.

BOTH VUL.   DEALER SOUTH

West	North	East	South
			1♠
pass	2♠	pass	4♠[1]
all pass			

1. Might have rebid 3NT which North should pass.

Opening lead: ♡Q

North
♠ 10 7 5 4
♡ A 4 3
♢ J 4 2
♣ K 8 5

West
♠ 9 2
♡ Q J 9 2
♢ K 10 6
♣ Q 7 4 2

East
♠ 6 3
♡ 10 8 5
♢ A 9 7 5
♣ J 10 9 3

South
♠ A K Q J 8
♡ K 7 6
♢ Q 8 3
♣ A 6

Here's your checklist:

1. You have a trump suit that allows you to draw trumps and still have at least one trump in each hand (unless you run into a 4-0 trump split and I wouldn't do that to you on the first hand!).
2. You have a nauseating off-limits suit, diamonds.
3. You have a side suit, clubs, that can easily be stripped by playing the ace-king and ruffing a club.
4. You have an equal-length side suit, hearts, that has an inevitable loser.

Basically you are looking at four possible red-suit losers: one heart and three diamonds. However, if you can force the opponents to lead diamonds...

Once the criteria have been met, this is the basic technique you should adopt:

1. Draw trumps.
2. Strip or eliminate the no-loser side suit, clubs, by playing the ace-king and ruffing a club.
3. Use the equal-length side suit with the inevitable loser to throw the opponents in, eliminating the suit from both your hand and dummy in one fell swoop. In other words, after having won the

Sometimes you have to coordinate steps #1 and #2 as entry problems may require you to use your trump suit to help you strip a side suit. Patience.

opening lead with the ♡K, you are eventually going to play the ace and a heart.

4. Sit back and enjoy the fruits of your labor. The player who wins the heart exit must either break diamonds or give you a ruff and a sluff. Either return costs the defense a trick. Well done.

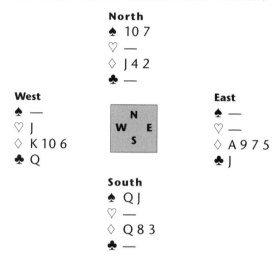

North
♠ 10 7
♡ —
◊ J 4 2
♣ —

West
♠ —
♡ J
◊ K 10 6
♣ Q

East
♠ —
♡ —
◊ A 9 7 5
♣ J

South
♠ Q J
♡ —
◊ Q 8 3
♣ —

Just to give you another look at the magic, this is the position after West has been throw in with a heart. Notice there are no more hearts or clubs in either your hand or dummy — those suits have been stripped. No matter what West leads, you will only lose two more tricks. If West leads a club or a heart, ruff in dummy and discard a diamond from your hand. If West exits a diamond, play second hand low and you can lose no more than two diamond tricks.

The remainder of the chapter deals with variations on this theme, but the bottom line is always the same: *remove all the safe exit cards from the player who is about to be thrown in.*

Not every throw-in play is made using an equal-length side suit. At times the throw-in suit is the trump suit itself. The trick is to give up your inevitable trump loser at just the right moment.

A **safe exit card** is any card a defender can lead that does not cost a trick. It may not gain a trick, but it doesn't cost a trick and that can be very important.

NEITHER VUL.   DEALER SOUTH

West	North	East	South
			1NT
pass	2♣	pass	2♡
pass	4♡	all pass	

Opening lead: ♣Q

North
- ♠ K 4 3
- ♡ K 8 5 4
- ◇ A J 7 6
- ♣ 8 7

West
- ♠ Q 10 8 6
- ♡ J 9
- ◇ 10 5 2
- ♣ Q J 9 2

East
- ♠ A 9 2
- ♡ Q 10 2
- ◇ 4 3
- ♣ 10 6 5 4 3

South (You)
- ♠ J 7 5
- ♡ A 7 6 3
- ◇ K Q 9 8
- ♣ A K

Your overview tells you:

1. You have an off-limits spade suit.

2. You have one trump loser with a normal 3-2 (68%) break.

3. You have two equally divided side minor suits that have no losers.

4. There will be no long suit establishment.

In order to force a spade lead from an opponent, use your trump loser to your advantage. Win the opening lead, and take the ace and king of hearts, leaving the high trump at large. Now cash a second club, stripping that suit, and begin to strip diamonds.

If East trumps the third diamond, East will either have to lead a spade (giving dummy a free trick with the ♠K), or lead a club, conceding a ruff and a sluff, which also costs a trick. East has no answer. If East refuses to trump the third diamond, exit with a trump to force a black-suit return. Once East leads a 'black' the most you can lose is two more tricks.

When stripping two side suits (clubs and diamonds), strip the shorter one first (clubs). If you strip diamonds before clubs, East can ruff the third diamond and exit safely with a club (not a ruff and a sluff at this point) forcing you to broach spades.

Throwing an opponent in using an **unequal** length side suit (say Ax in your hand facing xxx in the dummy) doesn't cut the mustard. The player being thrown in will have a safe exit in that very same suit because the suit has not been stripped from both hands. There is a way to get around this — 'evening' out the throw-in suit. Let's look at an example.

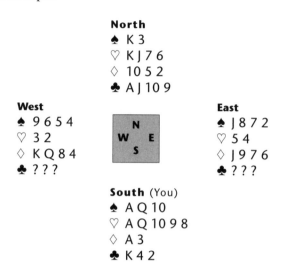

North
♠ K 3
♡ K J 7 6
◇ 10 5 2
♣ A J 10 9

West
♠ 9 6 5 4
♡ 3 2
◇ K Q 8 4
♣ ? ? ?

East
♠ J 8 7 2
♡ 5 4
◇ J 9 7 6
♣ ? ? ?

South (You)
♠ A Q 10
♡ A Q 10 9 8
◇ A 3
♣ K 4 2

BOTH VUL.		DEALER NORTH	
West	**North**	**East**	**South**
	1♣	pass	2♡
pass	3♡	pass	3♠[1]
pass	4♣[1]	pass	4◇[1]
pass	4♡[2]	pass	6♡
all pass			

1. Cuebid.
2. Minimum opening bid.

Opening lead: ◇K

If you attack clubs and get them right, you make seven, but if you get them wrong, down you go in six because they will cash a diamond... But why guess the club suit? If you can throw the opponents in and force a club play, wouldn't that be better?

Win the diamond lead, draw trumps, and play three rounds of spades, discarding a diamond from dummy. Suddenly diamonds is an equally divided suit; there is one diamond in each hand. Diamonds is now a perfect candidate to be your throw-in suit: exit a diamond and claim. Whoever wins must either lead a club or give you a ruff and a sluff.

Evening out a side suit makes it possible to use that suit as a throw-in suit.

How good are you at resisting temptation?

		EAST-WEST VUL.	DEALER: SOUTH
West	**North**	**East**	**South**
			1NT
pass	2♡¹	pass	3♠²
pass	6♠	all pass	

1. Transfer.
2. Four spades with extras.

Opening lead: ♠2

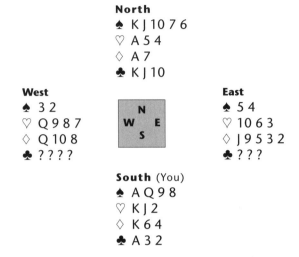

North
♠ K J 10 7 6
♡ A 5 4
◇ A 7
♣ K J 10

West
♠ 3 2
♡ Q 9 8 7
◇ Q 10 8
♣ ? ? ? ?

East
♠ 5 4
♡ 10 6 3
◇ J 9 5 3 2
♣ ? ? ?

South (You)
♠ A Q 9 8
♡ K J 2
◇ K 6 4
♣ A 3 2

West leads a passive trump and East follows. Who should you play for the ♣Q?

That is a trick question, of course. It doesn't matter who has the ♣Q! Your contract is cold. If you draw trumps, strip diamonds, and use hearts as your throw-in suit by playing the ace, the king and then the jack, you can force a club play. The problem is that some players (not you, of course) may not be able to resist the temptation of taking the heart finesse. If it loses and a heart comes back, your slam now depends upon finding the ♣Q. But, if you use hearts as your throw-in suit, the slam is on ice. If your hearts were Kxx instead of KJx, it would be easier to think of hearts as a throw-in suit.

When you have two equally divided side suits, both missing a queen, either of which can serve as a throw-in suit to force a lead in the other, use the weaker of the two suits (hearts) to force a lead in the stronger (clubs).

Something new is about to be added. In all the previous examples you threw an opponent in with one suit to force that opponent to lead another. But sometimes you only have losers in one suit. This should be considered your off-limits suit. In this case, you are going to have to attack the suit, the bad news. The good news is that you *will* strip the hand before you attack your off-limits suit.

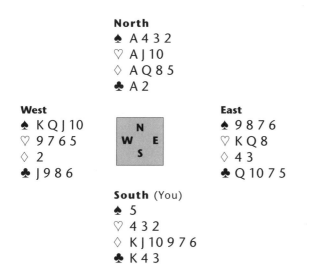

North
♠ A 4 3 2
♡ A J 10
♢ A Q 8 5
♣ A 2

West
♠ K Q J 10
♡ 9 7 6 5
♢ 2
♣ J 9 8 6

East
♠ 9 8 7 6
♡ K Q 8
♢ 4 3
♣ Q 10 7 5

South (You)
♠ 5
♡ 4 3 2
♢ K J 10 9 7 6
♣ K 4 3

BOTH VUL.		DEALER SOUTH	
West	**North**	**East**	**South**
			2♢[1]
pass	6♢	pass	pass[2]
all pass			

1. Weak.
2. This man can't take a joke.

Opening lead: ♠K

You have losers in one suit, hearts. Translation; you are going to have to lead hearts first (the bad news). However, this hand can be stripped (the good news, right?). You can ruff three spades in your hand, one club in dummy, and still arrange to end up in your hand in order to lead a heart to the ten. It goes without saying that you must also draw trumps, leaving at least one trump in each hand in the process.

Win the ♠A, ruff a spade; cross to dummy with a trump and ruff another spade. Return to dummy with a second trump, strip clubs (the ruff putting you in dummy), and trump dummy's last spade, completing the stripping process. Now lead a heart to the ten and queen. East is endplayed.

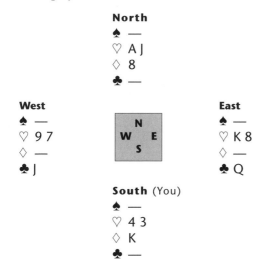

North
♠ —
♡ A J
♢ 8
♣ —

West
♠ —
♡ 9 7
♢ —
♣ J

East
♠ —
♡ K 8
♢ —
♣ Q

South (You)
♠ —
♡ 4 3
♢ K
♣ —

A heart return goes into the A-J while a black suit lead is a ruff and a sluff. Had you carelessly taken two heart finesses without stripping the hand, the opponents would have chalked up 100 points instead of you chalking up 1370 points.

At times you may have what appears to be an inevitable side-suit loser even though you and partner jointly have the ace-king of the suit. For example, Axx in one hand facing Kxx in the other; perhaps AKx facing xxxx, even AKxxx facing xxx.

There may be a way to eliminate this loser without discarding it on a long suit winner from another suit. The following example shows you how it is done.

NEITHER VUL.		DEALER:SOUTH	
West	**North**	**East**	**South**
			1♠
pass	4NT[1]	pass	5♣[2]
pass	6♠	all pass	

1. RKB for spades.
2. Two key cards including the ♠Q.

Opening lead: ♣10

North
♠ A 10 6 5
♡ A K 8 7 6
♢ Q
♣ K Q J

West
♠ 3
♡ Q 10 5
♢ J 9 8 4 2
♣ 10 9 8 7

```
    N
  W   E
    S
```

East
♠ 4 2
♡ J 9
♢ A 10 7 6 5 3
♣ 4 3 2

South (You)
♠ K Q J 9 8 7
♡ 4 3 2
♢ K
♣ A 6 5

Even though you are staring at two losers, you can hardly blame your partner for carrying on to slam. The bad news, of course, is that disgusting wastage in the diamond suit, 5HCP down the drain. But there is some compensating good news: diamonds is an equally divided side suit. Whenever you see an equally divided side suit with an inevitable loser(s), think throw-in!

Draw trumps, strip clubs, play the ace and king of hearts (key plays), and exit a romantic diamond, the king and queen going down the tubes together. If the player who has the ◇A is heartless (has no more hearts) you are about to be presented with a ruff and a sluff. This, in turn, allows you to discard a heart from your hand while ruffing in dummy.

This example adds a new dimension to the strip-and-endplay. If you can manage stripping opponent A (East) of a suit even though opponent B (West) remains with a winner in that suit, you will pre-vail if you can throw opponent A in after the hand has been stripped or partially stripped.

Here is yet another variation of a strip and throw-in:

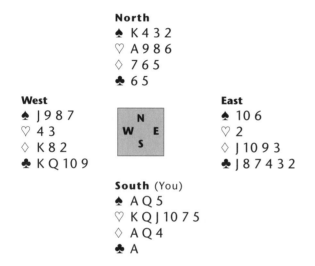

North
♠ K 4 3 2
♡ A 9 8 6
♢ 7 6 5
♣ 6 5

West
♠ J 9 8 7
♡ 4 3
♢ K 8 2
♣ K Q 10 9

East
♠ 10 6
♡ 2
♢ J 10 9 3
♣ J 8 7 4 3 2

South (You)
♠ A Q 5
♡ K Q J 10 7 5
♢ A Q 4
♣ A

		DEALER SOUTH	
BOTH VUL.			
West	**North**	**East**	**South**
			2♣
pass	2♠[1]	pass	3♡
pass	4♡[2]	pass	6♡
all pass			

1. Three controls: one ace and one king or three kings.
2. Natural.

Opening lead: ♣K

Time for an overview. You see that you have loser(s) in only one suit, diamonds, the off-limits suit. Furthermore, if spades divide 3-3, you can discard a diamond on a spade and take the diamond finesse for an overtrick. Normally, when you have losers in just one suit, you strip the hand and attack that suit. But something new is about to be added: you may be able to force West to lead a diamond smack into your A-Q (or give you a ruff and a sluff if he prefers).

At Tricks 2 and 3, draw trumps ending in dummy and ruff a club, stripping that suit. Next, test the spades. When you play the ace, queen, and king of spades, you notice that spades do not break 3-3 and that West is the one with the spade length. Now suppose you lead dummy's last spade and discard a diamond, a loser in any case. This is a neat form of a loser-on-loser play that gains you a trick. West, now on lead, must either lead a diamond into your A-Q or a club, giving you a ruff and sluff. If a club is returned, ruff in dummy and discard the ◊Q, discarding from the short side of the off-limits suit.

At times you can use the suit you are stripping as your throw-in suit. When you play the fourth round of spades, discard a certain diamond loser instead of ruffing. As West is about to take the trick, West is effectively endplayed. A diamond lead goes smack into your AQ, and a ruff and a sluff allows you to ruff in dummy while diposing of the ◊Q from your hand. You have just pulled off a combination loser-on-loser and throw-in play at the same time.

When given a ruff and a sluff, discard from the short side of the 'off-limits' suit and ruff on the other side.

Practice hands

Hand 1 *Temptations and Off-limits Suits*

BOTH VUL.   DEALER SOUTH

West	North	East	South
			1NT
pass	2♣	pass	2♠
pass	4♠	all pass	

Opening lead: ♡Q

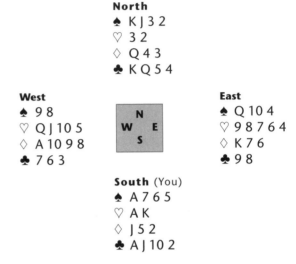

North
♠ K J 3 2
♡ 3 2
♢ Q 4 3
♣ K Q 5 4

West
♠ 9 8
♡ Q J 10 5
♢ A 10 9 8
♣ 7 6 3

East
♠ Q 10 4
♡ 9 8 7 6 4
♢ K 7 6
♣ 9 8

South (You)
♠ A 7 6 5
♡ A K
♢ J 5 2
♣ A J 10 2

You may or may not have any trump losers, but you are likely to have three diamond losers if you have to lead the suit first, or two if they do. Diamonds is clearly an off-limits suit. What you have to do is pretend that the ♠J in dummy is a small spade and play the ♠AK early. If the ♠Q drops, so much the better: you can draw a third trump, strip the hand, and attack diamonds yourself, probably losing three diamond tricks. However, if the ♠Q doesn't drop, you can use it as your throw-in card and get the trick back because you can force a favorable return. The order of plays after winning the opening lead should be: ♠AK leaving the ♠Q at large, second heart winner, stripping the shorter side suit first. If East refuses to ruff the third club, toss East in with a spade and wait for a favorable red-suit return. If you finesse the ♠J and it loses to East, East will have safe exit cards in hearts, clubs, or perhaps a third spade. Now you will have to attack diamonds yourself. Not pretty.

Key points
- When an outstanding high trump can be used as a throw-in card, there may not be such an urgency to take a trump finesse. If you don't take the finesse, you have the best of both worlds: if the missing honor drops, you have no trump loser; if it doesn't, use your trump loser as a throw-in card after you strip the hand.
- When stripping two suits (here clubs and hearts) strip the shorter combined suit first (here hearts before clubs).

Hand 2

North
♠ A 7 6
♡ J 4 3
♢ K Q 10
♣ A J 6 5

West
♠ K Q 10 9
♡ A Q
♢ 9 7 4 3 2
♣ 4 3

East
♠ J 8 4 3 2
♡ K 10 9 8
♢ J 6 5
♣ 2

South (You)
♠ 5
♡ 7 6 5 2
♢ A 8
♣ K Q 10 9 8 7

BOTH VUL.		DEALER NORTH	
West	**North**	**East**	**South**
	1NT	pass	2♣
pass	2♢	pass	3♣
pass	4♣	pass	5♣
all pass			

Opening lead: ♠K

You wind up in 5♣, having cleverly bypassed the frigid 3NT — part-ner's fault, of course. West leads the ♠K, and the hand looks hope-less. Even though you can discard one heart on a diamond, you are left with three heart losers — or are you? Since your only losers are in hearts, you must attack hearts first. Is there any hope? Yes, but only if you strip the hand before you lead a heart.

Win the ♠A, ruff a spade, draw trumps, strip diamonds, discarding a heart, and ruff dummy's last spade. Spades and diamonds are both stripped, trumps have been removed, you have trump in both hands, your table is set; lead a heart and see what happens.

Even though the defenders have the ace, king and queen of hearts, they can only take two heart tricks because the suit is blocked. After West wins the queen and ace, West must lead a diamond or a spade giving you a ruff and a sluff, so you make your contract after all. Never give up.

Key point
- With losers in only one suit, no matter how anemic that suit appears, strip the hand before playing the suit. The suit may be blocked or the opponents may be friendly enough to block it for you!

EAST-WEST VUL.   DEALER SOUTH

West	North	East	South
			1♠
pass	2NT[1]	pass	3♡[2]
pass	4♠[3]	all pass	

1. Jacoby 2NT – an artificial spade raise.
2. Singleton.
3. Lack of interest (wasted ♡K).

Opening lead: ♡Q

Many players use the Jacoby 2NT convention in response to a major-suit opening bid to show opening bid values with at least four-card trump support plus no side-suit singleton or void. Opener then rebids a singleton, or has various other options with no short suit. The downside of the convention is that you lose your natural 2NT response.

If upon winning the club your opponent elects to give you a ruff and a sluff, discard a diamond from dummy, the hand that is shorter in the off-limits suit, and ruff in your hand. Next, enter dummy with a trump and lead up to your ♦K, going for an overtrick.

Hand 3

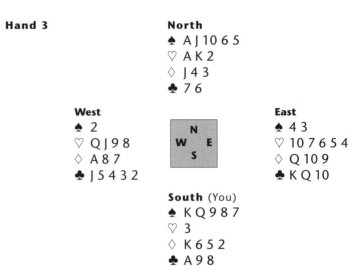

North
- ♠ A J 10 6 5
- ♡ A K 2
- ♦ J 4 3
- ♣ 7 6

West
- ♠ 2
- ♡ Q J 9 8
- ♦ A 8 7
- ♣ J 5 4 3 2

East
- ♠ 4 3
- ♡ 10 7 6 5 4
- ♦ Q 10 9
- ♣ K Q 10

South (You)
- ♠ K Q 9 8 7
- ♡ 3
- ♦ K 6 5 2
- ♣ A 9 8

You have a certain club loser and three possible diamond losers. Diamonds is clearly an off-limits suit. If you attack diamonds, the normal play is low to the king, and if that loses, you lead low to the jack. As it happens, this would result here in the loss of three diamond tricks. However, if you can force either opponent to lead a diamond, you only lose two diamond tricks. What you would like to do is throw them in with a club, say, after stripping hearts, and force a diamond return. The problem is that clubs is not an equally divided side suit. Throwing opponents in with unequally divided suits usually doesn't work. They can exit with that suit safely, forcing you to trump. But you can make clubs an equally divided suit.

Win the opening lead, draw trump ending in dummy, play a second high heart, discarding a club, and ruff a heart. Clubs is now an equally divided side suit. Play the ace and another club and force a diamond return (or a ruff and a sluff). You wind up losing two diamonds and one club.

Key point
- When presented with a ruff and a sluff, discard from the hand that is shorter in the off-limits suit, and trump in the other hand. Amen.

Hand 4

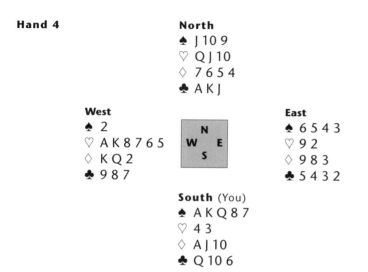

North
♠ J 10 9
♡ Q J 10
♢ 7 6 5 4
♣ A K J

West
♠ 2
♡ A K 8 7 6 5
♢ K Q 2
♣ 9 8 7

East
♠ 6 5 4 3
♡ 9 2
♢ 9 8 3
♣ 5 4 3 2

South (You)
♠ A K Q 8 7
♡ 4 3
♢ A J 10
♣ Q 10 6

NORTH-SOUTH VUL. DEALER WEST

West	North	East	South
1♡	pass	pass	dbl
2♡	2NT	pass	3♠
pass	4♠	all pass	

Opening lead: ♡A

West continues with the king of hearts and another heart. East ruffs the third heart and you overruff. Your only losers are in diamonds, but there is an overwhelming probability that West has both diamond honors. As ever, whenever you have losers in one suit only, strip the hand before you play that suit. Say you draw two rounds of trumps and West discards a heart on the second round. At this point, dummy and East each have one trump while you have two. If you draw the last trump and then finesse in diamonds, West will win and have a safe exit in hearts or clubs (since there will be no trumps in dummy). There must be something better. There is — a **partial strip**.

After drawing two rounds of trumps, leaving East with a trump (East is not going to get in), cash three club winners ending in dummy and lead a diamond to the ten and queen. Too bad East can't hand over his trump, a safe exit card, to West. As it is, West either has to lead a diamond into your A-J or surrender a ruff and a sluff, allowing you to trump in dummy while discarding your ♢J. Now you can enter your hand with the ♢A, draw East's last trump, and chalk up another well-played hand.

Key point
- Although one of the keys to a strip-and-endplay is to throw an opponent on lead while you have at least one trump in each hand and neither opponent has a trump, a partial strip (leaving one opponent with one or more trumps) may work. If *the player being thrown in* does not have a safe trump exit, you may still gain a trick on the return. It may be your only chance.

Test yourself

Armed with these techniques (maybe you should review them once more!), you should be ready for this five-problem quiz.

NEITHER VUL.		DEALER NORTH	
West	**North**	**East**	**South**
	1♣	pass	1♠
pass	2♠	pass	4♠
all pass			

Opening lead: ◊K

1.

North (Dummy)
♠ Q J 10 7
♡ J 8 7 5
◊ A 2
♣ K Q 2

South (You)
♠ A K 5 3 2
♡ Q 3 2
◊ J 9
♣ A 5 3

Solution on page 215

Plan the play (spades are 2-2).

NEITHER VUL.		DEALER NORTH	
West	**North**	**East**	**South**
	1♣	pass	1♡
pass	2♡	pass	4♡
all pass			

Opening lead: ♠10

2.

North
♠ A 2
♡ K 5 4 3
◊ 8 6 4
♣ A J 10 7

South (You)
♠ K Q J
♡ A 9 8 7 6
◊ J 3
♣ K 9 8

Solution on page 216

You win the spade ace in dummy and play the king and ace of hearts, West discarding a high diamond on the second heart. Plan the play from here.

3.

North
- ♠ 9 8 7 3 2
- ♡ A 2
- ◇ K J 3
- ♣ 4 3 2

```
    N
W       E
    S
```

South (You)
- ♠ A K Q J 10 6
- ♡ Q 3
- ◇ A 8 2
- ♣ A K

Plan the play.

		BOTH VUL.		DEALER SOUTH	
West	**North**	**East**	**South**
			2♣
pass	2◇[1]	pass	2♠
pass	3♠[2]	pass	4♣[3]
pass	4♡[3]	dbl	pass
pass	5◇[3]	pass	6♠
all pass			

1. Waiting.
2. Positive.
3. Cuebid.

Opening lead: ♡5

Solution on page 217

4.

North
- ♠ 6 4 2
- ♡ A 10 9
- ◇ K 10 9 8
- ♣ A 5 2

```
    N
W       E
    S
```

South (You)
- ♠ A Q 8
- ♡ 6
- ◇ A Q J 6 5 4
- ♣ K Q J

East plays the ♡2 (standard signals). Plan the play.

		BOTH VUL.		DEALER SOUTH	
West	**North**	**East**	**South**
			1◇
2♡	2NT	pass	3♡[1]
pass	4♣[2]	pass	4◇
pass	4♡[2]	pass	6◇
all pass			

1. Game forcing cuebid - usually shows shortness.
2. Cuebid.

Opening lead: ♡K

Solution on page 218

NORTH-SOUTH VUL.   DEALER WEST

West	North	East	South
1♡	dbl	pass	4♠
all pass			

Opening lead: ♡A

5.

North
♠ A J 4 2
♡ Q 8
♢ J 3
♣ A Q 7 4 2

```
    N
 W     E
    S
```

South (You)
♠ K Q 10 9 7 3
♡ J 10
♢ A 10
♣ 6 5 3

Solution on page 219

West continues with the ♡K, East playing first the ♡3 and then the ♡6. At Trick 3, West shifts to the ♢K. Plan the play.

Test yourself — solutions

1.

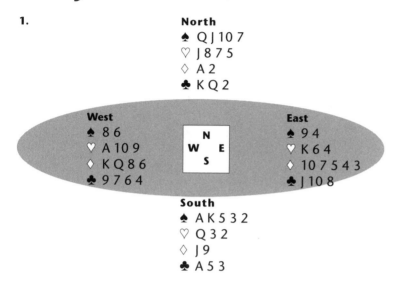

North
- ♠ Q J 10 7
- ♡ J 8 7 5
- ◇ A 2
- ♣ K Q 2

West
- ♠ 8 6
- ♡ A 10 9
- ◇ K Q 8 6
- ♣ 9 7 6 4

East
- ♠ 9 4
- ♡ K 6 4
- ◇ 10 7 5 4 3
- ♣ J 10 8

South
- ♠ A K 5 3 2
- ♡ Q 3 2
- ◇ J 9
- ♣ A 5 3

NEITHER VUL.		DEALER NORTH	
West	**North**	**East**	**South**
	1♣	pass	1♠
pass	2♠	pass	4♠
all pass			

Trick 1: ◇K

You have losers in two suits, hearts and diamonds. Diamonds is an equally divided suit and hearts is an off-limits type suit. Win the ◇A, draw trumps, strip the clubs, and exit a diamond. West wins but has to break hearts, limiting your losses in that suit to two tricks. If West gives you a ruff and a sluff instead of leading a heart, ruff in dummy and discard a heart from your hand, the shorter side of the off-limits suit.

NEITHER VUL.		DEALER NORTH	
West	**North**	**East**	**South**
	1♣	pass	1♡
pass	2♡	pass	4♡
all pass			

2.

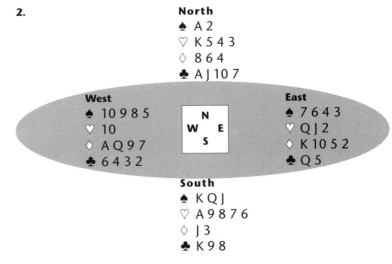

North
♠ A 2
♡ K 5 4 3
♢ 8 6 4
♣ A J 10 7

West
♠ 10 9 8 5
♡ 10
♢ A Q 9 7
♣ 6 4 3 2

East
♠ 7 6 4 3
♡ Q J 2
♢ K 10 5 2
♣ Q 5

South
♠ K Q J
♡ A 9 8 7 6
♢ J 3
♣ K 9 8

You would like to avoid the club guess, because if you get it wrong, down you go, losing two diamonds, a heart and a club. If you consider clubs an 'off-limits' suit, you can make the hand. Play two more high spades, discarding a diamond from dummy; you now have two diamonds in each hand. Exit a diamond. Let the opponents cash two diamonds and a heart, but when their fun and games are over, one of them will have to lead a club or give you a ruff-sluff and that's all she wrote.

3.

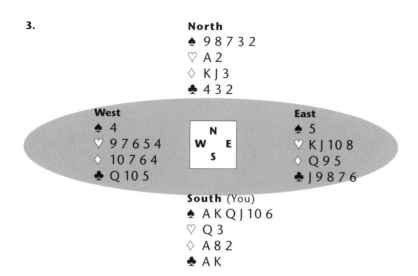

North
♠ 9 8 7 3 2
♡ A 2
♢ K J 3
♣ 4 3 2

West
♠ 4
♡ 9 7 6 5 4
♢ 10 7 6 4
♣ Q 10 5

East
♠ 5
♡ K J 10 8
♢ Q 9 5
♣ J 9 8 7 6

South (You)
♠ A K Q J 10 6
♡ Q 3
♢ A 8 2
♣ A K

BOTH VUL.		DEALER SOUTH	
West	**North**	**East**	**South**
			2♣
pass	2♢[1]	pass	2♠
pass	3♠[2]	pass	4♣[3]
pass	4♡	dbl	pass
pass	5♢[3]	pass	6♠
all pass			

1. Waiting.
2. Positive.
3. Cuebid.

Trick 1: ♡5 ?

You have a heart loser and a possible diamond loser, both of these being equal length suits. The double of 4♡ has pinpointed the ♡K, so use hearts as your throw-in suit to force a diamond lead from East.

Win the ♡A, draw trumps, strip clubs (making sure to trump the last small club in your hand), and exit a heart. East wins, but has to lead a diamond from the queen (or give you a ruff and a sluff). Slam made, thank you very much.

BOTH VUL.		DEALER SOUTH	
West	**North**	**East**	**South**
			1◊
2♡	2NT	pass	3♡[1]
pass	4♣[2]	pass	4◊
pass	4♡[2]	pass	6◊
all pass			

1. Game forcing cuebid - usually shows shortness.
2. Cuebid.

Trick 1: ♡K ♡A ♡2 ♡6

4.

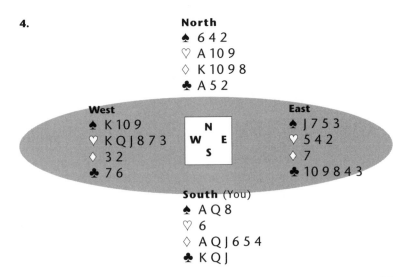

North
♠ 6 4 2
♡ A 10 9
◊ K 10 9 8
♣ A 5 2

West
♠ K 10 9
♡ K Q J 8 7 3
◊ 3 2
♣ 7 6

East
♠ J 7 5 3
♡ 5 4 2
◊ 7
♣ 10 9 8 4 3

South (You)
♠ A Q 8
♡ 6
◊ A Q J 6 5 4
♣ K Q J

You have losers in only one suit, spades, so normally you would have to attack spades first. However, the heart suit offers alluring throw-in possibilities if West started with ♡KQJ.

Say you win the ♡A, ruff a heart, draw trumps, cash three rounds of clubs (completing the strip in both minors) ending in dummy, and lead the ♡10. If East plays low, as expected, discard the ♣8, a loser-on-loser play, giving West the lead. What can West do? A spade return goes into the ♠ A-Q, while a heart return, a ruff and a sluff, allows you to ruff in dummy while discarding the ♠Q.

After a hand has been stripped and declarer is finally forced to lead an off-limits suit, 'second hand high' with 10xx(x), Jxx(x) or Qxx(x) might be mandatory depending on the number of tricks needed. Second hand does this to prevent declarer from ducking the trick into partner's hand.

If East plays the ♡J (rats), ruff, enter dummy and lead a spade, hoping East plays low in which case you can insert the ♠8, once again endplaying West. However, a strong East player in this position would play the ♠J. If East does that, find yourself a softer game.

5.

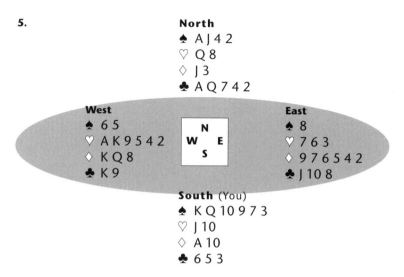

North
♠ A J 4 2
♡ Q 8
◇ J 3
♣ A Q 7 4 2

West
♠ 6 5
♡ A K 9 5 4 2
◇ K Q 8
♣ K 9

East
♠ 8
♡ 7 6 3
◇ 9 7 6 5 4 2
♣ J 10 8

South (You)
♠ K Q 10 9 7 3
♡ J 10
◇ A 10
♣ 6 5 3

NORTH-SOUTH VUL.   DEALER WEST

West	North	East	South
1♡	dbl	pass	4♠
all pass			

Trick 1: ♡A ♡8 ♡3 ♡10
Trick 2: ♡K ♡Q ♡6 ♡J
Trick 3: ◇K

It doesn't look good, does it? However, there is a chance. What you have to do is win the ◇A, your equal length suit, draw trumps, finesse the club queen, cash the ace of clubs, and exit a diamond to West's queen. If West started with one or two clubs headed by the king, West has no clubs left while East has a club winner. However, it is West who has the lead with the ◇Q, not East. Your partial strip of the club suit, your only chance, has worked! West must give you a ruff and sluff! Cheers!

Key ideas from Chapter 6

- Contracts that allow you to draw trumps while keeping at least one trump in each hand offer decided advantages to the declaring side.
- When neither you nor dummy has a long side suit that can be established to discard losers, and you have a suit you would rather the opponents lead, think **strip-and-endplay** to force a lead in that suit, your 'off-limits' suit.
- **Stripping** a suit means either (1) removing that suit from both your hand and the dummy, or (2) removing that suit from both opponents.
- In order to force a favorable lead from an opponent, it is necessary to remove that opponent's safe exit cards first. Stripping the trumps and non-loser side suits first is what must be done.
- A **partial strip** means removing a side suit or the trump suit from only one opponent and then throwing that opponent in.
- When an opponent leads a stripped suit (which gives declarer a ruff and a sluff), that play usually costs the defense one trick.
- When presented with a **ruff and a sluff**, discard from the short side of your 'off-limits' suit, and trump from the other.
- Equally-divided side suits with sure losers offer wonderful throw-in possibilities to force leads in off-limits suits. Of course, the hand must be stripped first.
- Even though your side suit may not be divided equally in the first place, you might be able to make it so by discarding a card from the longer side on a winner. Once it becomes an equal-length side suit, it can be used as your **throw-in suit**.
- When one opponent has the high trump, the trump suit can also be used as your throw-in suit to force a favorable return. As ever, the hand must be stripped first.
- At times you can use a **loser-on-loser play** as your throw-in card. Instead of trumping a card which would strip the suit, discard a loser instead. This assumes that the player who wins the trick will have to give you a trick in return.
- When you have only one suit that has losers, strip the hand before you attack that suit. *Just do it!*

MORE BRIDGE TITLES FROM MASTER POINT PRESS

ABTA Book of the Year Award Winners

25 Bridge Conventions You Should Know
by Barbara Seagram and Marc Smith
(foreword by Eddie Kantar)
192pp., PB   Can $19.95   US $15.95

Eddie Kantar teaches Modern Bridge Defense
Eddie Kantar teaches Advanced Bridge Defense
by Eddie Kantar
each 240pp., PB   Can $27.95   US $19.95

Also available in Interactive CD-ROM Editions
Modern Bridge Defense   Can $69.95   US $49.95
Advanced Bridge Defense   Can $69.95   US $49.95

The Bridge Technique Series
by David Bird & Marc Smith
each 64pp. PB   Can $7.95   US $5.95

Deceptive Card Play	**Planning in Suit Contracts**
Defensive Signaling	**Reading the Cards**
Eliminations and Throw-Ins	**Safety Plays**
Entry Management	**Squeezes for Everyone**
Planning in Defense	**Tricks with Finesses**
Planning in Notrump Contracts	**Tricks with Trumps**

Around the World in 80 Hands by Zia Mahmood with David Burn
256pp., PB   Can $22.95   US $16.95

A Study in Silver *A second collection of bridge stories* by David Silver
128pp., PB   Can $12.95   US$ 9.95

Becoming a Bridge Expert by Frank Stewart
300pp., PB   Can $27.95   US $19.95

Best of Bridge Today Digest
by Matthew and Pamela Granovetter
192pp., PB   Can $19.95   US $14.95

Bridge Problems for a New Millennium by Julian Pottage
160pp., PB   Can $14.95   US $11.95

Bridge the Silver Way by David Silver and Tim Bourke
192pp., PB   Can $19.95   US $14.95

Bridge Squeezes for Everyone* *Yes, even you*! by David Bird
220pp., PB   Can $24.95   US $17.95

Bridge: 25 Steps to Learning 2/1 by Paul Thurston (foreword by Eric Kokish)
192pp., PB   Can $19.95 US $15.95

Bridge: 25 Ways to Compete in the Bidding.by
Barbara Seagram and Marc Smith
220pp., PB   Can $19.95 US $15.95

Bridge, Zia... and me by Michael Rosenberg (foreword by Zia Mahmood)
192pp., PB   Can $19.95 US $15.95

Challenge Your Declarer Play by Danny Roth
128pp., PB   Can $12.95 US $ 9.95

Classic Kantar *a collection of bridge humor* by Eddie Kantar
192pp., PB   Can $19.95 US $14.95

Competitive Bidding in the 21st Century by Marshall Miles
254pp., PB   Can $22.95 US. $16.95

Countdown to Winning Bridge by Tim Bourke and Marc Smith
192pp., PB   Can $19.95 US $14.95

Easier Done Than Said *Brilliancy at the Bridge Table* by Prakash K. Paranjape
128pp., PB   Can $15.95 US $12.95

For Love or Money *The Life of a Bridge Journalist* by Mark Horton and Brian Senior
189pp., PB   Can $22.95 US $16.95

Focus On Declarer Play by Danny Roth
128pp., PB   Can $12.95 US $9.95

Focus On Defence by Danny Roth
128pp., PB   Can $12.95 US $9.95

Focus On Bidding by Danny Roth
160pp., PB   Can $14.95 US $11.95

I Shot my Bridge Partner by Matthew Granovetter
384pp., PB   Can $19.95 US $14.95

Larry Cohen's Bidding Challenge by Larry Cohen
192pp., PB   Can $19.95 US $15.95

Murder at the Bridge Table by Matthew Granovetter
320pp., PB   Can $19.95 US $14.95

Partnership Bidding *a workbook* by Mary Paul
96pp., PB   Can $9.95 US $7.95

Playing with the Bridge Legends by Barnet Shenkin
(forewords by Zia and Michael Rosenberg)
240pp., PB   Can $24.95 US $17.95

The Pocket Guide to Bridge by Barbara Seagram and Ray Lee
64pp., PB   Can $9.95   US $7.95

Richelieu Plays Bridge by Robert F. MacKinnon
220pp., PB   Can $24.95   US $17.95

Saints and Sinners *The St. Titus Bridge Challenge* by David Bird & Tim Bourke
192pp., PB   Can $19.95   US $14.95

Samurai Bridge *A tale of old Japan* by Robert F. MacKinnon
256pp., PB   Can $ 22.95   US $16.95

Tales out of School *'Bridge 101' and other stories* by David Silver
(foreword by Dorothy Hayden Truscott)
128pp., PB   Can $ 12.95   US $9.95

The Bridge Magicians by Mark Horton and Radoslaw Kielbasinski
248pp., PB   Can $24.95   US $17.95

The Bridge Player's Bedside Book edited by Tony Forrester
256pp., HC   Can $27.95   US $19.95

The Bridge World's 'Test Your Play' by Jeff Rubens
164pp., PB   Can.$14.95   US $11.95

The Complete Book of BOLS Bridge Tips edited by Sally Brock
176pp., PB (photographs)   Can $24.95   US$17.95

There Must Be A Way... *52 challenging bridge hands* by Andrew Diosy
(foreword by Eddie Kantar)
96pp., PB   Can $9.95   US $9.95

Thinking on Defense *The art of visualization at bridge* by Jim Priebe
197pp., PB   Can $ 19.95   US $15.95

You Have to See This... *52 more challenging bridge problems*
by Andrew Diosy and Linda Lee
96pp., PB   Can $12.95   US $9.95

Win the Bermuda Bowl with Me by Jeff Meckstsroth and Marc Smith
188pp., PB   Can $24.95   US $17.95

World Class — *conversations with the bridge masters*
by Marc Smith
288pp., PB (photographs)   Can $24.95   US $17.95